T0328800

Cambridge Elements ≡

Elements on Women in the History of Philosophy
edited by
Jacqueline Broad
Monash University

NÍSIA FLORESTA

Nastassja Pugliese
Federal University of Rio de Janeiro

Shaftesbury Road, Cambridge CB2 8EA, United Kingdom

One Liberty Plaza, 20th Floor, New York, NY 10006, USA

477 Williamstown Road, Port Melbourne, VIC 3207, Australia

314–321, 3rd Floor, Plot 3, Splendor Forum, Jasola District Centre, New Delhi – 110025, India

103 Penang Road, #05–06/07, Visioncrest Commercial, Singapore 238467

Cambridge University Press is part of Cambridge University Press & Assessment, a department of the University of Cambridge.

We share the University's mission to contribute to society through the pursuit of education, learning and research at the highest international levels of excellence.

www.cambridge.org
Information on this title: www.cambridge.org/9781009124133

DOI: 10.1017/9781009127219

First published 2023

A catalogue record for this publication is available from the British Library.

ISBN 978-1-009-12413-3 Paperback
ISSN 2634-4645 (online)
ISSN 2634-4637 (print)

Nísia Floresta

Elements on Women in the History of Philosophy

DOI: 10.1017/9781009127219
First published online: June 2023

Nastassja Pugliese
Federal University of Rio de Janeiro

Author for correspondence: Nastassja Pugliese, nastassja.saramago@fe.ufrj.br

Abstract: This Element presents the philosophical contributions of Nísia Floresta, a feminist philosopher of education from the nineteenth century in early postcolonial Brazil, who defended abolition and Indigenous rights. Focusing on five central works (*Direitos, Lágrima, Opúsculo, Páginas,* and *Woman*), it shows that they are connected by a critique of colonialism grounded in feminist principles. Influenced by the practical Cartesianism of Poulain de la Barre through the pamphlets of Sophia, Floresta applies to social structures the feminist principle that reason has no gender, arguing that a nation's civilizational level depends on whether natural equality is expressed in terms of social rights. Describing the suffering experienced by women, Indigenous people, and the black enslaved population, she defends education as a strategy against colonialism. Education should therefore aim toward physical and intellectual emancipation, restoring the lost dignity of individuals. Floresta's works thus foreground slavery and colonization as events that shaped philosophical modernity.

Keywords: Nísia Floresta, Cartesianism, Latin American feminism, Mary Wollstonecraft, modern philosophy

ISBNs: 9781009124133 (PB), 9781009127219 (OC)
ISSNs: 2634-4645 (online), 2634-4637 (print)

Contents

1 A Woman Philosopher in Postcolonial Brazil

Known for a long time as "the translator of Mary Wollstonecraft," Nísia Floresta (1810–85) is a key voice in the defense of women's rights in postcolonial Latin America. Floresta was a Brazilian philosopher who dedicated most of her works to criticizing the culture of modern Europe and the habits that were inherited by Brazilian culture, showing the inconsistencies between Enlightenment theory and colonial practice. Her major concern was women's access to education, and she argued that as long as women were kept ignorant of their own intellectual and physical capacities they would continue to have limited capacity for action. Floresta's philosophical reflections on equality and dignity were not only developed out of conceptual interest, but from a close observation of the social dynamics of Brazil, a society that was structured under colonial rule and remained a colony of Portugal for more than 300 years.

At the time Floresta was writing, Brazil was not yet a republic, but had recently become independent (in 1822). Slavery was still a legal institution, the Indigenous population was not integrated into society (Indigenous peoples were not regarded as citizens), and women did not have access to public jobs or higher education. Rio de Janeiro was the capital of the Brazilian Empire and its urbanization came with various social problems quickly observed by Floresta, such as the surge in poor people and marginalized social groups. Floresta – as an exception – was a highly educated woman well versed in classical philosophy and in the political debates of her time who aimed to expose the difficulties of creating an equal society after colonization.

Nísia Floresta Brasileira Augusta is the pseudonym of Dionísia Gonçalves Pinto. In her poem, *A lágrima de um caeté* (1849), on the condition of the Indigenous Caeté group during the Praieira Revolt, she used another pseudonym, "Tellesilla," and on other occasions she signed simply as B.A. (Brasileira Augusta). A number of anonymous essays were later assumed to have been written by Floresta. Although she employed various pseudonyms, she came to be known simply as Nísia Floresta. Nísia is short for Dionísia, her first name; Floresta is the name of the ranch where she was born and raised in the town of Papari, Rio Grande do Norte. Brasileira Augusta is a combination of an homage to her second husband (Augusta being the female form of the name Augusto) and a self-styled title – "Brasileira Augusta" also means noble Brazilian woman. In choosing her pseudonym, Floresta adopted a similar strategy to the eighteen-century anonymous British writer who gave herself the title "Sophia, a person of quality," indicating that she was a person of high social status and moral qualities. Nísia Floresta published around ten books including educational essays, travel diaries, and autobiographical texts in Portuguese, Italian, and French, as well as many essays in the popular presses of her day. Her daughter Lívia translated one of her Italian essays – *La donna* (*Woman*) – into English as an homage to her mother. Floresta did not write in English and English was not a language taught at her school.

Nísia Floresta was born in 1810 when Brazil, a colony of the Kingdom of Portugal, had just become (in 1808) the seat of the Portuguese colonial empire. Brazil was hosting the Portuguese royal family who, in an act of self-exile on account of the Napoleonic invasion of Portugal, established themselves in Rio de Janeiro. By hosting the royal family, the colony became the center of operations for the Kingdom of Portugal, gaining a special quasi-noncolonial status. When Floresta died in France, in 1885, she was a 75-year-old learned lady who was part of the intellectual circles of the French salons. She died four years before the proclamation of the Brazilian Republic and three years before the abolition of slavery. With independence, Brazil was no longer a colony and became an independent empire, the Império do Brasil. From the beginning of independence to the constitution of the republic, a period that lasted for more than half the nineteenth century, the empire of Brazil was a parliamentary constitutional monarchy under the rule of emperors Dom Pedro I (who was also prince of Portugal) and Dom Pedro II,[1] his son, who was born in Brazil. This was a period of political turmoil that led to various popular revolts, one of which – the Revolução Praieira – was the topic of Floresta's Indigenist epic poem, *A lágrima de um caeté* ("The Tear of a Caeté," 1849). Floresta did not live to witness the abolition of slavery in Brazil, but, through her lifetime, preliminary laws that significantly changed the institution of slavery had been promulgated.[2]

The life of Dionísia Gonçalves Pinto, the woman behind the Nísia Floresta pseudonym, is full of interesting anecdotes. Floresta's father, Dionísio Pinto

---

[1] During Floresta's lifetime, Prince Dom Pedro I had disputed the Brazilian Empire with his father, King D. João VI, and was successful in declaring Brazilian independence from the Kingdom of Portugal in 1822. In 1826, D. João VI, the King of Portugal, passed away. D. Pedro I, the heir to the throne, was in Brazil acting as Emperor of the newly independent nation. However, in Portugal, D. Pedro I was declared king. Despite D. Pedro I's role in Brazilian independence, he continued to be the successor to the Portuguese throne and became King of Portugal while also being Emperor of Brazil. Having to make a choice, he abdicated the Portuguese throne and stayed in Brazil. Various popular revolts against Pedro I's authoritarianism were taking place. Some years later, Pedro I abdicated his Brazilian throne and went back to Portugal to regain his power, leaving his five-year-old son Pedro II to succeed him. As he was still a minor, a vacuum of power was created leading to a period of rebellion. D. Pedro II was declared able to govern when he turned fourteen and was then, as emperor, able to control the popular revolts.

[2] For example, the end of the Atlantic slave trade through the Eusébio de Queirós Law (1850) and other rules that paved the way for abolition such as the Free-Womb Law (1871) and the Sexagenarian Law (1884). The end of slavery came with the promulgation of the Golden Law on May 13, 1888, which abolished slavery in all forms.

Lisboa, was a Portuguese lawyer; Floresta's mother, Antônia Clara Freire, who was born in Brazil, was from a prominent family in the northeastern region. Antônia was a widow when she married Floresta's father and together they had four children. Dionísio and his household have been depicted in Henry Koster's *Travels in Brazil* (1816). Koster spent a day at the Floresta ranch and made notes about their customs in his diary:

> Papari is about five leagues from Cunhau. Senhor Dionisio introduced me to his lady; he is a native of Portugal, and she a Brazilian. They possessed a small piece of land in the valley, and appeared to be comfortably situated. Papari may contain about three hundred inhabitants very much scattered. In the course of this year, I afterwards heard, that many persons flocked to it from other parts, owing to the absolute want of provisions. I went down to the edge of the lake to see the fishermen arrive, the people of the valley had all assembled to receive them; it was quite a Billingsgate in miniature – save that the Portuguese language does not admit of swearing.
>
> We dined in Brazilian style, upon a table raised about six inches from the ground, around which we sat or rather laid down upon mats; we had no forks, and the knives, of which there were two or three, were intended merely to sever the larger pieces of meat – the fingers were to do the rest. I remained at Papari during one entire day, that my horses might have some respite, that I might purchase another from Senhor Dionisio, and on poor Julio's account, whose feet had begun to crack from the dryness of the sands. (Koster 1816, pp. 64–65)

Floresta's ranch is depicted as a large and comfortable property but the family had to move away due to popular revolts triggered by anti-Portuguese sentiment (Doria 1933, p. 16).[3] In 1828, Floresta's father was assassinated by Capitão-mor Uchôa Cavalcanti who was contracted to kill him. The assassination was ordered by a family that did not accept the verdict of a judge who ruled in favor of one of Dionísio's clients (Floresta 2001, p. 51). This loss, which happened when Floresta was eighteen years old, marked her for life. It is said that her father encouraged her education and she benefited from the books in his library. We have no information on where Floresta studied and how she was educated. Duarte (2019) notes that there was a Carmelite convent in her city which was very well known among local families, suggesting that she probably attended the school (p. 24).

Most of these accounts can be found in Floresta's autobiographical works, but others come from unknown sources that are hard to track and verify with evidence. For example, Floresta was allegedly married to Manuel Alexandre Seabra de Melo when she was only thirteen. After a couple of months she

---

[3] Two revolts that marked Floresta's family history were the Revolução Pernambucana and the Confederação do Equador.

decided to abandon her husband and go back to her parents' house. The family then moved to another state, Pernambuco, as Floresta was being charged with household abandonment. There is no document that proves this charge, as Duarte (2021, p. 25) affirms, only biographers' notes that were based on oral history. Floresta later married again – a young lawyer from the Olinda Law School, Manuel Augusto de Faria Rocha. He became the father of her children who were properly registered under Manuel Augusto's name. This suggests that the first marriage may have been annulled otherwise her children could not have been registered under the name of Floresta's second husband (Duarte 2021, p. 25). Manuel Augusto graduated in 1832 as part of the first group of students from the Olinda Law School, one of the earliest in Brazil. The family then moved to Porto Alegre and one year later Manuel Augusto, who was 25 years old, died, leaving Nísia Floresta with two young children. After this loss, Floresta moved to Rio de Janeiro with her mother, D. Antônia Clara Freire, and her children.

Living as a widow for most of her life, Floresta was an autonomous woman who raised her children and took care of her mother, worked as a school director and a writer, and traveled the world. A couple of years after translating *Woman Not Inferior* (from the anonymous Sophia), Floresta started her own school in Rio de Janeiro, the Colégio Augusto.[4] Here, she implemented a progressive curriculum which included various foreign languages such as Latin, Greek, Italian, and French. She also taught her students history and geography, offering an alternative to the formal learning that reduced women's education to utilitarian domestic apprenticeship. With a curriculum that defied the accepted norms, the Colégio Augusto received criticism in the press. It was said that, by learning Latin, the girls who had been instructed in Floresta's school were acquiring useless knowledge (*O Mercantil* 1847, p. 3, n. 17). During the years when she directed this school, Floresta wrote various educational essays including *Conselhos à minha filha* ("Advices to my Daughter," 1842), a book that she would later translate to Italian (1858).

At the end of 1849, Floresta embarked on a transatlantic ship, *Ville de Paris*, with her two young children and headed for Europe. After almost two months at sea, on December 24, 1849, they arrived in France. Floresta was thirty-nine years of age. She declared, for immigration purposes, that she was going to Paris. Floresta justified the move to Europe in *Fragments d'un ouvrage inédit: Notes biographiques*: "I came to Europe thinking about finding some distraction in a life of the mind" (Floresta 2001, p. 32) And, in the literature, we find two other hypotheses justifying why she left Brazil: it was either a medical

---

[4] There is evidence that Floresta ran other schools before the Colégio Augusto.

recommendation for the sake of her daughter's health or self-exile due to the repercussions of her political activities (Duarte 2019, pp. 82–83). On September 7, 1849, Lívia Augusta had a serious accident, falling from a horse. The doctor of the Court, Cândido Soares, recommended that Floresta should seek a "change of air" to help Lívia in her recovery (Câmara 1941, pp. 35–36). Almost a century later, an interpretation of this medical recommendation was put forward in the press, leading to an alternative explanation for her move:

> Dr. Soares may have acted in this way following the suggestion of those people who were interested in keeping Floresta away from Brazil. She was a woman who voiced feminism, abolition, and the Republic in 1849, and this naturally constituted some kind of nuisance for the safeguard of order in Imperial Brazil, still impacted by so many civil wars. Nísia Floresta probably was seen as a dangerous agitator in this society with a slavery system where women also lived under a kind of an enslavement in the patriarcal regime. (*O Correio da manhã* 1954, p. 8)

Floresta's move was probably motivated by both causes, her daughter's health and the need for a change of air for the whole family, including herself and her own self-development. After traveling to France in 1849, Floresta never lived in Brazil again, visiting her home country only twice for short periods of time. In *Trois ans en Italie* (1864) Floresta writes that the death of her mother Antônia Clara Freire in 1855 was an additional reason for her decision to stay away from Brazil. In *Trois ans* she repeated the maxim that had appeared previously in *Itinéraire d'un voyage en Allemagne* (1857): "Traveling is the safest and most useful way for easing a great pain" (Lúcio 1999, p. 255).

In Europe, Floresta had her own intellectual circle and was friends with Auguste Comte, the French positivist philosopher. In Paris, Floresta attended Comte's course on the General History of Humanity at the Cardinal Palace. Due to this friendship, Floresta is considered in the literature to have been a positivist thinker. However, Comte himself declared in a letter to Audiffrent on 29 March 1857 that Floresta had "all the indications of being a good disciple" if only he could "transform a little bit her metaphysical habits" (Floresta 1888b, p. 4). He also was hopeful that Floresta and her daughter would set up a positivist salon in Paris, but they never did.

Floresta traveled across Europe and wrote travel diaries in which she described the architecture and the history of the places she visited, interspersing these with critiques of European customs. These diaries are heavily biographical and are good sources of information about her life. In one of her travel diaries, she says that an Italian bishop recommended that her work *Conselhos à minha filha* be adopted by Italian schools (Lúcio 1999, p. 730). Floresta lived in

Europe for around 28 years, and in her intellectual circle we also find Georges Louis Duvernoy, Victor Hugo, Alexandre Dumas, and others. Almost all of Floresta's letters were lost in a shipwreck, so there is little to no information on the extent of her participation in French intellectual circles other than what she describes in her autobiographical works.

Floresta always wished to go back to Brazil, but she never lived in her homeland again.[5] While in Europe, she sent her writings to the Brazilian press to have them published there. The newspapers would tell people about her life and her whereabouts. Later in Floresta's life, an American newspaper devoted to Portuguese-speaking immigrants in New York published an essay on her life and works. In this essay, Floresta is described as "a rare Brazilian writer" (*O Novo Mundo: Periodico Illustrato do Progresso da Edade*, 1872). Her books were acclaimed and received reviews. After she died, Floresta was cited by classical Brazilian authors such as Monteiro Lobato, Luis Camara Cascudo, and Gilberto Freyre. The second biographical essay on Floresta appeared in 1899, in a collection on illustrious Brazilian women by Ignez Sabino, *Illustrious Women from Brazil (Mulheres illustres do Brazil)*. It was in 1941 that a book-length biography appeared: Adauto da Câmara described Floresta's life and work in *História de Nísia Floresta*.[6] The first modern edition of her works appeared only in 1989 when Peggy Sharpe wrote the introduction and notes to the republished version of *Opúsculo humanitário* (*Humanitarian Opuscule*) and Constância Lima Duarte wrote the introduction to *Direitos das mulheres e injustiça dos homens* (*Rights of Women and the Injustice of Men*). For a long time Floresta's works were either rare or lost and only now are they being digitized in world libraries and preserved. Moreover, the city where Floresta was born, Papari, is now named after her and is called Nísia Floresta, which is also home to a museum in homage to her.

Although she did not live her whole life in Brazil, Floresta closely followed events in the country, connecting them to European and North American history. Through her writings, it is clear that she was interested in global history in order to better understand the customs of the nation and its class struggles. The key topics in her writings are women's rights and women's education, the

---

[5] She paid a short visit to Brazil in 1852 but returned to France where she then lived. Floresta died and was buried in Rouen in 1885. Livia was buried next to her mother in the cemetery in Rouen. In 1954, the government of the state of Rio Grande do Norte in Brazil decided to pay homage to Floresta and demanded that her body be exhumed from the Rouen cemetery to be reburied in Brazilian soil. The Brazilian government celebrated the historical event with an official commemorative stamp and a memorial.

[6] Henrique Castriciano (1979, p. 138) also wrote a biographical essay in 1930 (reprinted in 1979) and Oliveira Lima (1919) wrote one in 1919. Roberto Seidel (1938) published a small book (46 pages) on Nísia Floresta's life and works.

abolition of slavery, and Indigenous' rights. The historical moment in which Floresta was writing is a key period in the construction of Brazilian identity. Floresta was an intellectual of the early postcolonial period, who focused her scientific and philosophical efforts on trying to find ways out of the noxious social, economic, and cultural effects of colonization. As the country had recently become independent in the early 1800s, her works are foundational for the nascent Brazilian intellectual tradition.

2 Beyond the "Brazilian Wollstonecraft" Myth

Although there has been an effort to recover her works in the past few decades, the pseudonym Nísia Floresta is still surrounded by myths and misinformation. Floresta has been characterized as the Brazilian translator of Wollstonecraft for more than a century, and is associated with Wollstonecraft both for the wrong and the right reasons. Her first publication, *Direitos das mulheres e injustiça dos homens* (1832), which she dedicated to Brazilian women and Brazilian male academics, is described by Floresta herself – on the book cover – as a free translation of a French version of "Mistriss [*sic*] Godwin's" work. As Mary Godwin was Mary Wollstonecraft's married name, and since her work was known (but probably not read by many) in Brazilian political and intellectual circles, *Direitos* was accepted as Floresta's free translation of Wollstonecraft's *Vindication of the Rights of Woman* (1792), even though the first translation of Wollstonecraft's *Vindication* to Brazilian Portuguese only appeared in the twenty-first century.[7] Nevertheless, Floresta's *Direitos* was the first feminist work to be published in Brazil and it contributed significantly to the spread of feminist ideas in the country and more widely in Latin America (Botting & Matthews 2014).

The recovery history of this book is a complex episode that illustrates Wollstonecraft's reception in Brazil and recent research opens space for the study of arguments inspired by practical Cartesianism in the development of Brazilian feminism. In the 1980s, Constância Duarte, a Brazilian scholar, discovered that *Direitos* was not a direct translation of Wollstonecraft's *Vindication* and suggested that Floresta's free translation was actually a free appropriation of Wollstonecraft's arguments. Duarte concluded that *Direitos* was Floresta's original work even though it was inspired by the British feminist icon. However, because the works of other women philosophers have also been buried in silence and misinformation, it was only in 1996 that Maria Lúcia Pallares-Burke found out that the text was neither an original creation by

---

[7] The translator of this first edition of Wollstonecrafts's *Vindication* to Brazilian Portuguese, published in 2016, is Ivania Pocinho Motta.

Floresta nor a translation of Wollstonecraft, but a literal translation of the first Sophia pamphlet, the *Woman Not Inferior to Man: Or, a Short and Modest Vindication of the Natural Right of the Fair-Sex* (1739).[8] Even more recently, Botting and Matthews (2014) discovered the volume that served as a source for Floresta's Portuguese translation: the French translation of Sophia's *Women Not Inferior* by César Gardeton. Botting and Matthews found out that in Gardeton's French translation, the source work was attributed to "Mistress Godwin," Mary Wollstonecraft.

Given the information now available, one cannot say that Floresta is the translator of Wollstonecraft's *Vindication*. It is also wrong to say that *Direitos* is Floresta's original work or even an original free adaptation (Duarte 1995, 2021). One also cannot say that Floresta intentionally attributed the authorship of *Direitos* to Wollstonecraft as a literary prank (Pallares-Burke 1996). The fact is that Floresta translated the first pamphlet of the anonymous Sophia (Pallares-Burke 1996), a text that was considered, for a long time, to be a plagiarism of Poulain de la Barre's *L'égalité des deux sexes* (Moore 1916) but is now interpreted as a version or an adaptation of the arguments present in the Cartesian-inspired text *L'égalité* with some original additions (O'Brien 2009, Leduc 2010, Broad 2022).

Floresta's *Direitos* is a translation to Portuguese (1832) of the French translation (1826) by César Gardeton of the first English pamphlet of the anonymous Sophia published in 1739 (Botting & Matthews 2014). Floresta offered a literal translation of this French translation with just a few vocabulary adaptations with respect to the French source text (Soares 2017). Since the Wollstonecraft–Floresta myth is still being widely spread, it is important to highlight the fact that Floresta translated Gardeton's version of the Sophia pamphlet with a great level of literality, so that we should assume them to be the same text in two different languages.

Soares (2017) argues that Floresta adapts the tone by simple translational operations that soften the meaning of more offensive words or expressions.

---

[8] Leduc (2015) notes that

> As to [Sophia]'s identity, it remains unknown. Some thought, yet without any proof, that it was a pen name used by Lady Mary Wortley Montagu (1689–1762) ... In 1964, Myra Reynolds had echoed another hypothesis suggesting that Lady [Sophia] Fermor (1721–1745), the daughter of Thomas, the Earl of Pomfret, and the second wife of Lord [John] Carteret, could be [Sophia] ... Doris Mary Stenton suggests that [Sophia] was a man: "unlikely that a woman who felt deeply about the exclusion of women from all professions would have written like the so-called Sophia. ... Another possibility is that the three writers were one and the same person since at the time it was a rhetorical game to write on both sides of a question." But she concludes that "It remains impossible to prove either that the author of the three pamphlets was one and the same person or to reveal [Sophia]'s and her adversary's identities." (pp. 16–18)

There is more work to be done on this topic, but I will offer a basic comparison for illustrative purposes. The titles give us the first and more immediate evidence for the literality between Gardeton's French and Floresta's Portuguese translation of the Sophia pamphlet: while the French title is *Les droits des femmes, et l'injustice des hommes; par Mistriss Godwin. Traduit librement de l'Anglais* in Portuguese, it is *Direitos das mulheres e injustiça dos homens, por Mistriss Godwin, traduzido livremente do Francês*. The general structure of the texts also serves as additional evidence. Gardeton's French translation contains an addition at the end, not translated by Floresta (*"augmenté d'un apologue: L'instruction sert aux femmes à trouver des maris"*). Floresta chose not to translate the addition authored by Gardeton (which, in English, would read "Education helps women to find husbands"). Finally, with respect to the arrangement of chapters, both the French (*Les droits*) and the Portuguese translations (*Direitos*) display a minor difference in structure – not in content – with respect to the *Woman Not Inferior* version printed in London in 1739, authored by the anonymous Sophia: while in *Woman Not Inferior* the first chapter is also the introduction, in Gardeton and Floresta the introduction comes before the first chapter. Also, in *Woman Not Inferior* the conclusion is numbered as chapter 8, while in Gardeton and Floresta the conclusion is unnumbered. Hence, in *Woman Not Inferior* there are eight chapters (including the introduction and conclusion) and in *Les droits/ Direitos* there are six chapters, plus the introduction and conclusion. *Direitos* has a dedication that is not present in *Woman Not Inferior* nor in *Les droits*. This brief comparison serves the purpose of furthering the argument that *Direitos* and *Les droits* are neither translations nor versions of Wollstonecraft's *Vindication*, but of the modern English pamphlet *Woman Not Inferior*.

It is not known why Gardeton, when translating the Sophia pamphlet from English to French, changed its title from *Woman Not Inferior* to *Les droites des femmes* and attributed its authorship to Wollstonecraft.[9] It is possible that Gardeton was either assuming freedom as a translator or that his source text was anonymous and he decided to attribute authorship on the basis of its content. Or it could be that the source text available to Gardeton was itself

---

[9] In one of the French translations of the Sophia pamphlets, *La femme n'est pas inférieure à l'homme: Traduit de l'anglois* (1750), credited to Madeleine de Puisieux, there is a handwritten note attributing authorship of the work to "Mistriss Godwin" (Wollstonecraft). In this volume, owned by the National Library of France (BNF), there is no mention of authorship of the content, of the translator, or of the publishing house. There is, however, information about the printing location, London, and there are handwritten notes attributing the authorship to "Mme. Godwin" and the translation to "the Puisieux" (either Philippe Florence or his wife Madeleine d'Arsant). Although there are other versions of this pamphlet with different titles (such as, for example, *Beauty's Triumph, Les triomphe des dammes*), the first vindicatory pamphlet of the anonymous Sophia is known by the title *Woman Not Inferior to Man*.

misattributed to Wollstonecraft – so that the misattribution of authorship was done by a third party. It is possible that there might be a lost version of the Sophia pamphlet with the title *Rights of Women and the Injustice of Men* that has been wrongfully attributed to Wollstonecraft by some editor and Gardeton translated the work literally, passing the mistaken attribution forward in his translation. What "free translation" means in each of these texts is a methodological problem still to be solved, since a freely translated text can mean either a literal translation with minor adaptations of vocabulary (as in Floresta's case) or an adaptation of the original text that entails some degree of change in the theoretical content (the anonymous Sophia's text in comparison to Poulain's, for instance). On the front page of Gardeton's volume, we read that he translated into French the eighth edition of the English text ("traduit librement de l'anglais, sur la huitième édition"). Hence, there is still a lot of archival work to be done to find out which eighth edition he possessed and at which point Wollstonecraft's name started to be associated with and attributed to the first Sophia pamphlet.[10]

Botting and Cronin (2014) describe Gardeton's translation as "the first 'fake' edition of Wollstonecraft's *Vindication*" that is "actually a pirated copy of a French edition of Sophia's 1739 *Woman not inferior to man*" (p. 316). But given that Gardeton translated it from the eighth edition, there is no evidence as yet that this French translator willingly created a fake copy of Wollstonecraft's *Vindication*. A similarity between the titles of the translated books could also be a possible cause for the mistaken attribution of authorship. As we have seen, the word "vindication" appears on the subtitle of the first of the Sophia pamphlets, which reads, *a Short and Modest Vindication of the Natural Right of the Fair-Sex*. Also, the titles of Wollstonecraft's and Sophia's works, when translated into French, were changed, and in the course of various editions the titles of these works ended up bearing some resemblance. Finally, these texts were sometimes translated and published with no mention of authorship or of the name of their translators, creating greater confusion. Botting and Cronin (2014) also state that the "educator Nísia Floresta unwittingly translates Gardeton's 'fake' edition of the *Rights of Woman*" which becomes "one of the founding documents of Brazilian feminism" (p. 316). They are correct in saying that Floresta did not know that she was not translating Wollstonecraft's *Vindication*. On this brief reception history, they consider the founding document of Brazilian feminism to be the introduction Floresta wrote in *Direitos*.

---

[10] See Botting 2012, Johnson 2020, and Bour 2022 on the reception history of Wollstonecraft in Europe and the translation history of the *Vindication*.

However, the introduction to the Portuguese text is a translation. Floresta's original addition is the dedication page. This "Dedication" is a justification for why Floresta translated that particular text, and it expresses her intention to promote women's rights and female education with that translation. Hence, although *Direitos* is not a text originally written by Floresta, it is uncontroversial that not only the dedication page but the book itself, as a translation, is a founding document of Brazilian feminism.

This communication of ideas from one culture to another by means of translations was an important factor in the spread of Enlightenment ideas, within Europe and outside, during the construction of new nations. Brazil, as a recently constructed nation, is characterized by this interlacing of cultures and languages given that, due to colonization and the forced and free immigration of the workforce, the country had to cope with a mixture of identities and languages. This interlacing is expressed in the material history of books such as *Direitos*, a work that exemplifies the intellectual transmission between countries and cultures. *Direitos* was the first book published by Floresta and the first ever published in Brazilian Portuguese on the specific topic of women's right to education. Being the – now known – pseudo-translator of Wollstonecraft and having become the voice of women's right to education in nineteenth-century Brazil, Floresta became a kind of "Brazilian Wollstonecraft."

For a further understanding of the association between Floresta and Wollstonecraft, it should be noted that a central point in this intricate story of cultural and linguistic translation is that Floresta herself never knew that the work she translated was not Wollstonecraft's *Vindication*. Instead, she thought that she was building on the legacy, as characterized by the Viscount of Cayru, of "the famous English woman Vollstonecraft [*sic*], who also wrote the work Rights of Women" (Brasil 1827, p. 533). Hence, one of the many questions still open for discussion in the literature is why Floresta decided to translate Wollstonecraft, in particular. Having carried out archival research, and following hints offered by Botting and Matthews (2014), I argue that with her 1832 translation Floresta was engaging with political discussions concerning the education of women that had happened a couple of years before in the Brazilian Senate. This Senatorial discussion preceded the promulgation of the first educational law in Brazil and represents a key historical link between Floresta and Wollstonecraft. It is an episode in the reception of Wollstonecraft in Latin America that shows how her name had significant power in shaping discussions concerning women's education.

The educational law, which represents the first consolidation of accepted views on education and gender in Brazil, was promulgated in 1827 and stipulated that girls and boys had to study in separate schools with different curricula. The idea was that girls should have fewer lessons in mathematics than boys, and were allowed to learn only the basic operations of arithmetic – addition, subtraction, division, and multiplication – so as to be able to help with household finances. Boys, on the contrary, learned decimals, fractions, proportions, advanced arithmetic, and geometry. The law – promulgated in the postcolonial period, five years after independence when Brazil was a self-standing empire, though not yet a republic – resulted from a debate in the Brazilian Senate which, at that time, was housed in Rio de Janeiro. The debate, documented and archived in the Brazilian National Library, was about whether young women should be allowed to have a scientific education or continue to have a practical education, useful for household matters. The senators all voted in favor of different instruction for girls and boys and defended limiting women's learning to practical education. One of the senators, the Viscount of Cayru, argued:

> It should suffice for girls our old rule: read, write, count. Let's not be singular and eccentric. God gave beards to men not to women ... The four operations are enough, since they are not outside their capacity and can be useful for life. Their use of reason is very ill developed for them to be able to understand and practice higher operations ... I am convinced that it is vain to fight against nature.[11] (Brasil 1827, p. 533)

The only senator to defend curricular equality was the Marquise of Santo Amaro (from Rio de Janeiro), with an argument that took inspiration from the spirit of the modern times and the protocol of European nations: "It is not in accordance to the lights of the times we live in that we do not facilitate Brazilian women the access to this knowledge [of higher level mathematics] ... In every learned nation instruction is being given to girls and I think we should adopt the same practice" (Brasil,1827, p. 533). At this point in the discussion, the argument about incommensurability among cultures appeared. Senator Viscount of Cayru reacted by saying that the "learned nations" cannot serve as an example for Brazil. He then argued that "this habit of studying hard, deviating from what nature has made them [women] to do and from the ends for which they were created, is a vanity that makes them laughable, as Molière has shown in the comedy *Les femmes savantes* (1672)" (Brasil,1827, p. 533). And he continued, using arguments that defended gendered reason and a natural inequality between men and women:

> I do not deny that there have been women with male capacities. ... They have been rarities in our species, however, and they were not moral examples. ... There had been women who had sailed the sea of politics, specially after the French Revolution. But from that it did not follow any good results. It suffices to name the famous English woman Volstoncraft [*sic*], who also wrote the

---

[11] All English translations are mine.

work *Rights of Women* … She was condemned for being unfaithful, with an accusation from her husband, and could not reestablish her reputation as she got married with another enthusiast, Godwin … If we continue in this path, we won't be taken by surprise if people start demanding women to be able to study at universities to become doctors. (Brasil 1827, p. 533) 1827, p. 533)

This senatorial debate illustrates the climate of public opinion at the time, as it was used to justify how Brazilian schools should be organized and orient the form of their instruction. This event happened five years before Floresta translated and published the first edition of *Direitos*. As someone who was interested in changing public opinion with respect to women's role in society, Floresta chose to translate a work that would redirect established opinion. According to the senator Viscount of Cayru, Wollstonecraft's *Vindication* was the book that would make people demand women's access to higher education; and it was exactly the kind of content Floresta was willing to engage with. This intention to help construct the philosophical foundations for women's right to equal education in Brazil is literally expressed on the dedication page of *Direitos*. Floresta dedicates the work to Brazilian women and male Brazilian academics, to whom she says: "I hope that one day, during a free time between the highly important works from the ministry, I hope you will act with justice towards our sex and if you do not make a metamorphosis of the current state of affairs, at least we will find a better luck, that you won't doubt we are deserving" (Floresta 1989b, p. 21).

Floresta laments being a poor translator and asks for forgiveness for her mistakes, which could explain why she called her work a "free translation." As we now know, she attributes to Wollstonecraft the authorship of the original work, reproducing the mistake that was present in the French volume she had in her possession. Although one might think Floresta called her own work a "free translation" due to her freedom as a translator to adapt some vocabulary, the textual evidence we have is that in the source text one can read "traduit librement." The fact is that Floresta is not and cannot therefore be called "the Brazilian translator of Wollstonecraft." From this point on in the recovery history of Floresta's works, it is imperative we recognize that Floresta is profoundly influenced by the arguments of the anonymous Sophia in so far as *Woman Not Inferior to Man* was the text she decided to translate and dedicate to Brazilian academics. The story further unfolds, as the British authors Sophia and Wollstonecraft did have a lot in common.

As O'Brien (2009) shows, Wollstonecraft was part of the women's Enlightenment movement in eighteenth-century Britain and was profoundly impacted by her older contemporary Catharine Macaulay, a philosopher who was associated with the Bluestocking Circle. As Pohl and Schellenberg (2003) explain, the Bluestockings were learned English women and men who gathered during the second half of the eighteenth century at the London salons hosted by Elizabeth Montagu and her friend Elizabeth Vesey. Catharine Macaulay was apparently too radical for the Bluestockings' taste (Green 2020). Although we do not know the identity of Sophia, her pamphlets were associated with the philosophical production of the Bluestockings, circulating and influencing their views on woman's morality. So there is a thread of influences that, through the Bluestockings, connects the Sophia pamphlets to Wollstonecraft. The Bluestocking Circle, Catharine Macaulay's association with the Bluestocking Circle, and Macaulay's influence on Wollstonecraft are facts that add to the explanation of why, at some point in the French translation of the first Sophia pamphlet, this originally anonymous text was wrongfully attributed to Wollstonecraft. Although the Sophia pamphlet was published much earlier than Wollstonecraft's *Vindication*, both vindicatory works were part of women's contribution to the eighteenth-century English Enlightenment. If we use the Bluestockings and the anonymous pamphlet as interpretation keys, we can find more ways to understand the thread of influence of the British Enlightenment across the globe, and connect Floresta and Wollstonecraft. As Broad (2019) argues, Wollstonecraft calls for the recognition and restoration of women's dignity, a vindication that appears in a number of texts of the early modern era, including the Sophia pamphlets.

A final point about the Floresta–Wollstonecraft connection: Floresta was a nineteenth-century philosopher who was a founding mother of Latin American feminism. She wrote many books that were translated into various languages and found a great readership during her lifetime. *Direitos* had three editions over the course of seven years, and *Lágrima* had two editions in the same year. Floresta was widely published and read, and her ideas helped to create a momentum for women's intellectual production in her country. Her first book influenced the debate on women's rights in Brazil and in Latin America, and helped to spread awareness and give voice to other women who had the same concerns. In Brazil – a country that saw the suffrage movement only in the 1930s – we can now find women publishing their views on the right to vote and to participate in public life in the press, inspired by the path that Floresta opened several generations ago. Pallares-Burke (2021) recognizes that this moment, opened up by Floresta through public discussion, is a version, perhaps smaller in scale compared to the European tradition, of the woman question in Brazil. These discussions led to the strenghtening of the republican movement in Brazil. Francisca Senhorinha Motta Diniz, for example, argues in the newspaper *O Sexo Feminino*, which she edited, that "the Age of Enlightenment, the 19th century, will not end before men convince themselves that more than half of the ills that oppress them are due to the lack of attention they give to the education of women" (Diniz 1873, p. 1). It is possible to map, in the Brazilian press of that time, a vindicatory movement by a group of women intellectuals publishing and publicly voicing their philosophical points of view, in which women were arguing for equality in what can be called a Brazilian women's Enlightenment.

Floresta, then, can be associated with Wollstonecraft for the right reasons. She had, in Brazil, a symbolic power similar to that which Wollstonecraft had in eighteenth-century England when she became the voice of women's rights. Floresta was criticized as immoral – she abandoned her first husband and married again – and she defended divorce in her writings. According to Botting and Matthews (2014), Floresta should be "seen as the most influential Latin American intellectual to disseminate Wollstonecraft's name for symbolic and political ends in her local engagement with the women's rights issue" (p. 64). The name of Wollstonecraft was spreading fast; she was also cited by Joaquim Manuel de Macedo in *A Moreninha*, a work that marked the start of the Brazilian Romanticism literary movement. Floresta not only helped to disseminate Wollstonecraft's name, but she also became a powerful force connecting the thread of intellectual production in the old and the new worlds, thus going beyond local engagement with women's rights issues.

Floresta is now part of the reception studies of Wollstonecraft, even if this influence is somehow distorted and the Wollstonecraftian connection is only indirect. For example, we can see the presence of Wollstonecraft in at least two of Floresta's works: in the educational essay *Fanny or the Model for the Ladies* and in her major work *Opúsculo*. In the first work, a fictional narrative on the moral education of women, the main character is Fanny, the same name as Wollstonecraft's older daughter. In the story, Fanny is an exemplary daughter who has to deal with the death of her father in a street revolt. Her duty as a daughter in this moment is to go to amid the gunfire to try to save her father, and to heal the wounded soldiers. Here we see Floresta trying to enter the imaginary of political activism surrounding Wollstonecraft, applying it to the political situation in Brazil where social unrest was continuous. The second reference to Wollstonecraft is in the *Opúsculo humanitário*, her main work. Floresta says "But let us leave to Wollstonecraft, Condorcet, Sièyés, Legouvé, etc. the defense of the rights of the sex. Our task is another one, and we believe a more convenient one to modern society: the education of women" (Floresta 1989a, p. 29). Whether offering a rhetorical move to captivate newspaper readers or actually differentiating between the defense of the education of women and the defense of the rights of women, Floresta distinguishes her goal from that of Wollstonecraft.

Moving beyond the Floresta–Wollstonecraft association, there is much more to say about Floresta and her own vindicatory works. Once we seriously consider that *Direitos* is a translation of Sophia's *Woman Not Inferior*, new research opens up. As *Direitos* is the first publication by Floresta, we can use it as a lens to analyze her later works. My understanding is that Floresta makes use of the practical Cartesianism expressed in *Woman Not Inferior* to develop her own critique of the application of Cartesian principles through the analysis of the mechanisms of colonization, and uses it as a background when proposing her own educational project. Through an analysis of the relationship between Sophia and the Cartesian philosopher Poulain de la Barre, Floresta's own engagement with Cartesianism becomes clearer.

3 Floresta: Translator of the Anonymous Sophia and Author of Her Own Vindicatory Works

The work *Woman Not Inferior to Man* is an early modern feminist pamphlet that has been considered as either plagiarism or as a partial translation of Poulain de la Barre's *L'égalité des deus sexes* (Moore 1916; Ferguson 1985; Clarke 2013). In recent comparative analyses, there is agreement that Sophia's piece is not plagiarism nor merely a partial translation of Poulain's *L'égalité*, but a version – or "free adaptation" of Poulain's work – with a more radical tone, an expansion of his theory of equality. O'Brien (2009) points out that Sophia undertakes a free adaptation from *L'égalité*, interspersing paragraphs with added quotations (O'Brien 2009, p. 17).[12] Leduc (2010, 2015) argues that although *Woman Not Inferior* can be located in the tradition of rewritings of Poulain's *L'égalité*, it contains original additions and vocabulary changes. Broad (2022) shows that the significant variations in Poulain's vocabulary by Sophia result in distinctive arguments in the pamphlet for women's rights. Leduc (2015) argues that Sophia changed the tone of Poulain's discourse, leading to a more radical or strident feminism and a negative opinion of men in general.

Mapping the concepts, Leduc shows that Sophia has "verbal audacity" (Leduc 2015, p. 34) as she uses "generous" to describe women and "ungenerous" to describe men, and adopts a political language of "tyranny" and "usurpation." Moreover, instead of using the word "subject" to describe women's

---

[12] O'Brien (2009) suggests that some of these quotations are from Rowe and Pope, with references to Boadicea, Queen Elizabeth I and Eliza (Elizabeth Carter) (p. 17). This first Sophia pamphlet includes a response to a misogynistic piece in *Commonsense: Or The Englishman's Journal* by Chesterfield. The misogynistic arguments in *Commonsense* are based on the writings of the Frenchman Jacques de Tourreil (Broad 2022, p. 45). O'Brien (2009) also shows that there is a similarity in tone between the first Sophia pamphlet and the sixth edition of Lady Mary Wortley Montagu's *The Nonsense of Common-Sense* (p. 17), and suggests that this lends support to the hypothesis that Sophia was Sophia Fermor, friend and correspondent of Mary Wortley Montagu.

condition as Poulain did, Sophia employs "enslaved" (Leduc 2015, p. 19). Whereas Leduc sees no improvement on Poulain's political ideas on natural rights in Sophia's pamphlet, Broad argues that Sophia builds on the Cartesian thesis found in Poulain to develop a more robust theory of natural equality and justification for the restoration of women's rights. In choosing to use the concepts "generous" and "ungenerous" to describe women and men, and using the vocabulary of "tyranny" and "usurpation" to describe men's unjustified power over women, Sophia is building on the notion of Cartesian generosity and offering a more forceful defense of the political participation of women (Broad 2022, p. 44).

Floresta, in turn, develops Sophia's appropriation of Poulain's practical Cartesianism. Floresta, like Sophia, uses the concept of generosity to talk about women's virtues and their superior moral capacities: "Be generous, my dear; generosity is a sublime sentiment, proper of a well formed soul; look for occasions to exercise it" (Floresta 1845, p. 23). Besides "generosity," Floresta also employs the language of charity (*caridade*), self-denial (*abnegação*), and care (*cuidado*). Charity is considered a sublime virtue that should be cultivated in women's hearts. In the *Opúsculo* we read: "Charity, this sublime virtue, that is never more dutifully exercised as when it [is] done through the hands of a woman" (Floresta 1989a, p. 35). And in *Woman* she reinforces this idea of charity as virtue proper of women: "Let the heart of woman be the seat of real charity and of all the human virtues" (Floresta 1995, p. 107).

Floresta also considers that women should recognize the political power that they hold in their roles as mothers, daughters, and wives. In these capacities, women can be exemplars of virtues through their caregiving abilities and they can choose self-sacrifice in order to serve nonegoistic purposes.

> But it is your self-abnegation, for the sake of their happiness and credit, that you must employ; and, above all, the great work of the future that you ought to keep in view, sacrificing to it even your own welfare, and all your amusements. This sublime sacrifice is expected of your generous hearts – of you, who alone can make or impose it. (Floresta 1995, p. 111)

When fostering the education of their sons, women can help minimize the possibility that they will become oppressors of women:

> The teaching of the equality, that ought to reign between man and woman, begins in them with their own little sisters in their childish games, and in the domestic habits through which transpire only too plainly the pride and pretension of the little boy, which are so amusing to you, but which, Oh women, constitute the germ of that presumptuous egotism, which oppresses you through life to the detriment of his own felicity. (Floresta 1995, p. 113)

When fostering the education of their daughters, a well-educated mother can help girls recognize their dignity: "A well-educated mother sufficiently instructed to conduct the education of her daughter will aways have the best advantages when directing her efforts with tenderness to inspire through example the experience of her own dignity" (Floresta 1989a, p. 91). Caring for offspring is a choice that gives women political power to form and contribute to the education of future citizens; more specifically, mothers can help raise nonegoistic men who will not oppress women. Floresta considers that care is a choice, and the most morally significant choice made by mothers, because she observes that women can decide not to care for their own offspring. Although her argument is in favor of care as a moral obligation, she grounds this obligation in the rational consciousness of women and the practice of virtues they cultivate through education.

> To be a mother, in the moral sense, is, not the having children, but the knowing how to educate them well ... Reflect, ye mothers; reflect on the responsibility imposed on you by that high title, that some of you bear so lightly, and with so little thought! Consider seriously the painful consequences, sometimes fatal, of your carelessness in educating your children, or incapacity for the task; consider, too, the happy effects were you all to dedicate yourselves to the maternal duties and the exercise of virtue. (Floresta 1995, p. 110)

Another change that Floresta makes to Sophia's text is with respect to the word "slave" (*escrava*). As we saw, this word appears in Sophia as an adaptation, stronger in tone than Poulain's use of the word "subject" to describe women's condition. Floresta adopts the word "slave" to describe the condition of women when, in the *Opúsculo humanitário*, she summarizes the arguments contained in *Direitos* (Floresta 1989a, p. 62). She also uses "slave" to characterize the way women are treated by men in the essay *Woman*: "Cease that silly talk with which you dazzle her reason, making her believe herself a queen where she is but the slave of your caprice. ... Man must abstain from considering woman as his toy or his slave, he must regard her as the companion of his life" (Floresta 1995, p. 102).

However, most of the occurrences of the word "slave" in *Opúsculo*, Floresta's central work, are used to describe black enslaved women. In the *Opúsculo* (Floresta 1989a, p. 93), Brazilian boys perceive their wet nurses as "a slave submissive to his caprices": the "miserable African woman who goes from the whip, in the correction houses or the house of their own masters (*senhores*), to the cradle of the innocent [boy] to offer him her milk" (Floresta 1989a, p. 93). The woman slave appears as the primary caregiver of Brazilian boys and girls. Their relationship is pictured as detrimental to moral and physical education: "We see children, when already able to make use of their own legs, spend most part of their days on the arms of different people from the family or of the women slaves designated by their parents" (Floresta 1989a, p. 121). This habit is used as an example of how slavery is not only an "atrocious crime" (Floresta 1989a, p. 151) but also a source of "pernicious lessons" (Floresta 1989a, p. 96) that lead to ingratitude and insensitivity:

> Since all the labor done inside the household is, among us, carried out by slaves, the young girl finds herself since her first infancy surrounded by so many pernicious lessons as there are occasions to witness the gestures, the words and actions of this unfortunate race, demoralized by captivity and condemned to the education of the whip! . . . Her nascent sensitivity gradually gets used to this distressing spectacle, which is daily repeated in front of her; it is not rare to see her (we say this with sorrow) inflicting the most cruel treatment to the wet-nurse that cared for her. (Floresta 1989a, p. 96)

This change in usage of the term "slave" shows Floresta's understanding of the different conditions among women, and is evidence that she wants to distinguish the domestic conditions of white women – who hold a greater level of political power – from that of the black enslaved women and Indigenous women. Floresta calls white women who are limited to the household "patrícias" (patricians) or "senhoras" (ladies), rarely calling them slaves.

Floresta maintains the language of equality and tyranny found in Sophia, but adds to her works the conceptual pairing of civilization and barbarism to express how inequality is a result of tyrannical governments and cultures: "From the discretion of tyrannical oppressors that in the name of the heavens came to take away the goods that heavens bestowed upon us! . . . Taking away our simple and modest customs, in exchange they gave us fraud and lies, calling us barbarians – the name that they take from their own ancient and modern history" (Floresta 1989a, p. 144).

The awareness of the arbitrary power of settlers is described as a source of revolt for anyone who knows these historical facts: "the philosopher, the Christian, who knows the history of our Brazil cannot refrain himself from revolting against the abuses of the civilization of his European settlers, inherited by their successors" (Floresta 1989a, p. 145). Floresta is also aware of and interested in economic disparity and the language of social class. She talks about the "poor women" and "the poor class" (Floresta 1989a, p. 124), arguing for the importance of building a strong working class that includes paid women workers. Floresta also criticizes the idea of the so-called "natural laziness" of Indigenous women who perform the same work as "poor woman from the city," yet neither are recognized for their work (Floresta 1989a, p. 150).

While she is critical of the barbarisms of colonization, Floresta does not ignore European culture. In the *Opúsculo*, for example, she constructs a short history of

Western civilization based on women's roles and achievements in the so-called great civilizations. In doing so, she engages with European philosophers such as Rousseau, Condorcet, Montesquieu, Fénelon, and others. A central point of agreement among researchers on the Sophia pamphlets and on Poulain is the influence of Descartes on both Poulain's *L'égalité* and Sophia's *Woman Not Inferior*. Poulain is an important figure in the history of feminism and, as a "thoroughgoing Cartesian" (Schmitter 2018, p. 1), he employs doctrines such as dualism, skeptical doubt, and accounts of the passions in developing his arguments concerning women's rational capacities and educational conditions (Reuter 2019). Poulain is less interested in offering an interpretation or an evaluation of Cartesian doctrines than he is in applying his metaphysics and philosophical method to the problem of gender differences. It is due to this methodology in *L'égalité* that scholars map the tradition of Cartesian feminism, practical Cartesianism, or social Cartesianism onto various early modern texts.[13] Poulain's *L'égalité* and Sophia's *Woman Not Inferior,* its English adaptation, are both examples of how Cartesian doctrines shaped modern feminism. Since Floresta's first work is a translation of the anonymous Sophia pamphlet, Cartesian doctrines also influenced Brazilian and Latin American discussions on gender.

Floresta cites a great number of other philosophers that she engages with, and further studies on these influences and criticisms need to be conducted. Sophia's influences also go beyond Descartes and some of these have already been traced. Broad (2022) shows that Sophia's distinctive arguments are influenced by Locke's views on arbitrary power. The Sophia pamphlet, a work written in England at the time of the Bluestocking movement, absorbs influences from women intellectuals in eighteenth-century England. This influence can be seen, for example, when Sophia cites Eliza, the bluestocking Elizabeth Carter (O'Brien 2009, p. 17), especially in the articulation between domestic space and political power present in the introduction and first chapter of the pamphlet. Although authorship of the pamphlet is still unknown, speculation revolves around women who participated in the English salons, such as Lady Mary Wortley Montagu (1689–1762) and Lady Sophia Fermor (1724–45). Another attribution is to Madame d'Arsant de Puisieux (1720–98), given that The National Library of France categorizes a French translation of the Sophia pamphlet as the work of Madeleine d'Arsant de Puisieux (1750).[14]

---

[13] All these labels are ways in which Cartesian principles and doctrines are applied beyond Cartesian texts and, from extra exegetical interests, used as instruments in the analysis of various practical questions.

[14] However, the text itself is anonymous and the translation is not signed. Madame d'Arsant is most probably the translator because the text is dated 1750, although this is an open debate (Garnier 1987). See notes 4 and 6 for further information on the authorship of the Sophia pamphlet and its various copies.

The relationship between Floresta and Descartes, then, is mediated by Sophia's appropriation of Poulain's Cartesianism. Clearly, there are other sources of influence on both Sophia's and Floresta's works; however, I have a reason for limiting my interpretation to the impact of Cartesian feminism on Floresta. Although Descartes's name is not mentioned in the source texts, *L'égalité* and *Woman Not Inferior*, Floresta explicitly cites Descartes in the *Opúsculo humanitário* as the person responsible for opening a new era in philosophy for women: "After Descartes has opened a new era to philosophy . . ., the French women no longer remained limited to the examples of courage given by Joanne of Arc when she had the glory of freeing her homeland, . . . other virtues, other triumphs, of which women are more deserving, took place, distinguishing the French women of our days" (Floresta 1989a, p. 31).

Following this recognition, Floresta lists a number of women that she considers to have been able to flourish – intellectually and philosophically – as a result of the spread of Cartesianism in France: Madame de Sevigné (Marie de Rabutin-Chantal, 1626–96); Madame de Maintenon (Françoise d'Aubigné, 1635–1719); Countess of Genlis (Stéphanie-Felicité du Crest de Saint-Aubin, 1746–1830); Madame de Campan (Jeanne Genet, 1752–1822); Madame Necker (Albertine-Adrienne de Saussure, 1766 – 1841); Madame Tastu (Sabie Voïart, 1798–1885); Madame de Gizot (Pauline de Meulan, 1773–1827); Madame de Stäel (Anne-Louise Germaine de Stäel-Holstein, 1766–1817); and George Sand (Amandine Aurore Lucile Dupin, 1804–76).

Floresta never knew that she had translated Sophia and offered a Cartesian-inspired feminist manifesto to Brazilian society. Because the Sophia pamphlet's translation into Portuguese was Floresta's first published work, and a work for which she gained recognition as a public intellectual, the philosophical arguments presented in *Direitos* act as important interpretation keys for her other works. More specifically, I maintain that in the *Opúsculo* Floresta puts practical Cartesianism to the test by analyzing how modern civilizations do not mirror the natural equality advanced by Enlightenment thinkers, and most especially, by showing how colonization is at odds with the principle of natural equality resulting from Cartesian dualism – that is, the equality that human beings bear among each other because they are all rational creatures and, in this sense, share the same essence. Floresta does this by highlighting the inconsistencies between Enlightenment theory and colonial practice, arguing that social relations should properly mirror the natural equality of all human beings. Following *Direitos*, she develops her views on the civilization and education of women in the *Opúsculo humanitário* and then describes the injustices of the colonial system in *Lágrima* and *Páginas*.

Floresta applies the structure of *Direitos das mulheres e injustiça dos homens* to her own reflections, making it a method of investigation: all of Floresta's writings are either about the rights of women (*direitos das mulheres*) or a critique of the injustices of men (*injustiça dos homens*). The way she does this in philosophical terms is by developing Cartesian feminism into a kind of Cartesian anti-colonialism or Cartesian abolitionism. The main Cartesian thesis that is at work in Floresta's thought is that intelligence has no sex,[15] a consequence of mind–body dualism, that is, the view that mind and body are distinct substances. She derives a couple of corollaries from this metaphysical principle. If intelligence has no sex, and men and women are intellectual equals, then the observed differences in intellectual production are due to unequal access to education. Moreover, this can and should be remediated by means of a significant change in school curricula for girls in order to give women a scientific education, thus preparing the ground for a wider public presence. If intelligence has no sex and intellectual differences are the result of social structures that prevent women from developing and gaining recognition for their intellectual pursuits, then the natural equality of the sexes should be better reflected in civil law and social practices. Among other things, Floresta argues for a politics of memory building, where the stories of women from the past who contributed to what she calls "the progress of civilization" are told and honored (Floresta 1989a, p. 12)

> The ardent desire ... to see our country among the progressive nations, imposes on us the obligation of analyzing frankly and impartially the education of women in Brazil in the hopes of inspiring, with our example, writers with more ability than ours to write about a subject that has been so much neglected among us. ... We are not motivated by the vain desire to operate a reform in the spirit of our country since we know that it will take many years perhaps centuries to erase inherited prejudices that will allow such metamorphoses. We hope only that the zealous workers of the edifice of civilisation in our land be attentive to the examples that history offers us, as to how essential it is for the nations to strengthen their own happiness, to associate to women this important work. (Floresta 1989a, p. 50)

Floresta argues that neglect of history, and the history of women, comes from Portuguese culture which disregarded its own great men; citing verses from the poet Almeida Garrett (Floresta 1989a, p. 51), she shows that the Portuguese do not show recognition for their distinguished citizens through monuments or posthumous homages. She says that she will do justice and pay homage to

---

[15] Descartes does not use the word "intelligence;" rather, he uses "mind." Floresta probably uses "intelligence" because she is willing to make not only a metaphysical claim about the natural equality in rational capacities between men and women, but also an epistemological claim.

ancestors, citing important Portuguese writers, having referred to important women in former chapters.

But Floresta does not stop there. If she did, she would be like many of her contemporaries and the women Cartesians who came before her, defending equality of the sexes and seeing education as a strategy for safeguarding women's rights. Floresta extends Poulain's and Sophia's radical interpretation of the natural equality of the sexes to race, geography, and culture. Poulain and Sophia map the prejudices that follow from considering the minds of women to be different to those of men, arguing from a Cartesian point of view that reason is a defining trait of human existence. In her turn, Floresta defies the limits of practical Cartesianism by looking at Brazilian postcolonial culture and social structures, pointing out that not only women but Indigenous people and the black enslaved population experience the same lack of recognition of their existence as human beings. Indigenous people and the black enslaved population are not treated as equals and, at a deeper level, are excluded from the pool of beings that are seen as complete – perfect – human beings, fully deserving of rights and dignity. In a colonial state, Indigenous and black enslaved populations suffer violence, their very existence is in constant peril, and the preservation of their cultural legacy is in danger. For Floresta, this situation has its roots in an incomplete application of the principle of equality – which is observed only toward a few – leading to a cycle of suffering and injustice that is built into the social structure. Education is then thought of as a complex instrument that can restore the lost dignity of individuals with a half-human status. Building from her observations, Floresta denounces the fact that the black enslaved population are treated as "automatons" or as "work-animals" (Floresta 1989a, p. 116).

To show how her social analysis derives from a radical interpretation of equality, I will offer an overview of key arguments in Floresta's major works: *Lágrima, Páginas, Opúsculo*, and *Woman*.

3.1 *A lágrima de um caeté* (1849)

A lágrima de um caeté, which sold out all three of its editions during Floresta's lifetime, is a long poem on the sufferings of the Indigenous population. The title means "the tear of a Caeté," the name of an Indigenous nation considered to be extinct. In the poem, Floresta describes European colonizers as part of a tyrannic nation who pretend to be free and to hold humanistic values, but are violent and inhumane, invading someone else's lands. The Indigenous character in the book, although nameless, is continually described as a full human being – conscious of himself as a mind and a body, conscious of his social group – who is in peril, both as an individual and as a tradition bearer. The Europeans are characterized as being far removed from the ideals of humanism, but they are always expected to act humanistically or rationally; the domination of Indigenous nations finds absolutely no justification. This is the first time that Floresta shifts the meaning of civilized versus barbarian, applying to the colonizers the label of barbarians (Floresta 2021a, p. 17). She struggles to claim that Indigenous people are civilized, although their will of vengeance is called "a noble will," as it is the will to defend their own existence. In the poem, Floresta demonstrates that Indigenous people have no social status. They could be either savages or civilized but their situation is such that they are neither one nor the other. They are not savages, because their natural goods, their belonging to wild nature, is no longer in their possession as they have been expropriated from their lands. Yet, they are not civilized, because "the civilized" kept "their tools of destruction far away from them" (Floresta 2021a, p. 18) – these tools being weapons and books. Indigenous people have neither guns nor degrees. Floresta concludes that Indigenous people must listen to the "Reality" – she uses a capital R to describe it – that they have lost the fight against the invaders and should run to the forests to protect themselves, their dignity, and their freedom. Throughout the poem, the Indigenous Caeté has a voice; he speaks in the first person, he has a fervent inner life, and he acts rationally. This is not a heroic view of Indigenous struggle, however, and Floresta is unable to conceive of a conciliatory solution for their situation. It is a poem about the tear of a soon-to-be extinct nation.

3.2 *Páginas de uma vida obscura* (1854)

Páginas is a collection of essays published in the newspaper *O Brasil Ilustrado* in eight chapters (March 14 and 31, April 15 and 30, May 15 and 31, June 15 and 30) signed with the initials B. A. In this narrative, there is an introduction in which Floresta shows the importance of telling the stories of common people – those who are not warriors or geniuses or rich, but simple everyday people who, as random examples, represent the life of a group. In the prelude, she asks her readers to kneel down by the grave of a slave to learn from his life – and his death – what virtue really is. Floresta narrates the story of a Congolese man forced into slavery in Brazil, who goes through life without being able to keep his family together, is displaced from one place to another when sold, is unable to keep his community ties, and, even in the face of suffering, decides not to take revenge. Domingos, the enslaved man, is an exemplar because he has a "spiritual superiority" (Floresta 2019, p. 141),[16] and is "elevated above his

---

[16] Since there is no modern edition of *Páginas de uma vida obscura* and each chapter is published in a long list of separate facsimiles of nineteenth-century newspapers, I made use of the work of Sergio Barcelos Ximenes (2019) who independently transcribed *Páginas* and other works of Floresta, reproducing them in *Cinco Obras Completas de Nísia Floresta Brasileira Augusta*.

tyrants" (Floresta 2019, p. 144). Floresta highlights his dedication and self-sacrifice when confronting moral challenges. The goal of her descriptions of the life of the mind and spirit of an enslaved person is to show him as an equal and, in a sense, as a superior moral being who should be dignified when he is in fact being treated with contempt. She says, "not even the church prays for them after their passing" (Floresta 2019, p. 137). But she is going to be the one to elevate slaves as a group by singing the virtues of this common slave. In this book, Floresta characterizes slavery as "the monstrous child of despotism" (Floresta 2019, p. 139), "the infamous libel of the Christians" (Floresta 2019, p. 139), "the anomaly of great people" (Floresta 2019, p. 139), "the anti-humanitarian system" (Floresta 2019, p. 141), and points to slavery as the single most salient contradiction of the Enlightenment, of civilization, and of republicanism. For Floresta, slavery is an indication that Europeans are republicans in name only, as they have a ferocious love for absolutism and servitude.

3.3 *Opúsculo humanitário* (1853)

Opúsculo humanitário is Floresta's main work, with the clearest and most explicit philosophical arguments. The book's chapters were published as separate essays in two newspapers *Diário do Rio de Janeiro* (with no indication of authorship) and *O Liberal* (using the pseudonym "B.A.") in 1853 and 1854. The essays were collected in a book with sixty-two chapters. The book starts with a brief history of women and a list of women from the past, with the aim of justifying the thesis that women's education is a measure of civilization; that is, that the level of social justice in a given society can be objectively measured by women's access to high-quality, scientific education. Floresta then argues that natural equality among human beings should be mirrored in civil equality, consolidating the readings that appeared in previous works. The key strategy for transforming civil society and dealing with the problem of equality is to treat education as a triad – an event that depends on cultural habits, families, and schools or educational institutions – and to think of its goal as that of preventing the cycle of violence that reproduces itself through the social structures of a postcolonial society.

A key objective of education is to restore the lost dignity of individuals – to recognize their full humanity, their capacity for thinking, and their ability to experience emotions (to suffer, to love, to have compassion) and to exercise their will for the sake of the common good. This objective is achieved when there is recognition of human dignity and this dignity is preserved and valued by means of virtuous habits and just laws. In chapter LIX of *Opúsculo humanitário*, Floresta proposes the preservation of Indigenous customs in

Brazilian culture and argues that schools and families should teach everyone the importance of Indigenous habits such as breastfeeding and community engagement. With respect to the black enslaved population, Floresta argues against slavery, describing suffering and violence and mapping the way violence is reproduced beyond the relationship between slave owners and enslaved people. Floresta is hopeful for abolition, and considers that the development of a working class will aid the social integration of the black population into Brazilian society – they would be financially recognized for their invaluable participation in building the new country (an independent Brazil).

3.4 *Woman* (1859)

Woman is a long essay originally written in Italian, entitled *La donna*, and published as a chapter in Floresta's book *Scintille d'un'anima brasiliana* (1859). It was translated into English by her daughter, Lívia Farias, in 1865. The essay is a critique of modern European morals combining the major theses found in *Direitos*, *Lágrima*, *Opúsculo*, and *Páginas,* but with two additions: the tone found in her moral educational writings[17] and the strategy of reverse anthropology present in her travel writings.[18] It starts by describing two ladies going on a trip on the Strasburg railway to a village twenty leagues (around sixty miles or ninety-six kilometers) from Paris. Later in the text, Floresta discloses that she is talking about herself and a friend. The purpose of the trip is to go to an unnamed poor hamlet hidden among the trees to try to find the granddaughter of Floresta's friend. The baby girl's mother had died and she had been thrust by her father onto "strange nurses in some out-of-the-way village where you never go yourself" (Floresta 1995, p. 6). Floresta went there with the baby's grandmother to see how the girl was being treated. When they arrived, they were shocked by the poor conditions and saw that a child was actually taking care of the baby (and other babies that were sent to the house). The baby

---

[17] Floresta wrote various works on women's virtues and women's moral education (*Conselhos à minha Filha, Discurso às Educandas, Fanny*) that elaborate on the social conditions of women in the nineteenth century, both in Brazil and in Europe. They offer both a descriptive and a prescriptive evaluation of women's proper virtues.

[18] British social anthropology is known for its fieldwork expeditions to the colonies (in the work of Malinowski and Evans-Pritchard, for example) as part of an ethnological methodology that allows anthropologists, through comparison, to make general inferences about culture and human social organizations. The standard of cultural development was taken to be Europe and its customs. The act of going to the colonies to be exposed to the different and the exotic, and treating non-European societies as living examples of some form of culture that Europeans had overcome through progress, is what I refer to here as the social anthropological method. Floresta reverses social anthropology, because she is a native of what they would consider to be a less-developed culture, and offers a critical analysis of European culture.

had been entrusted to foster care by the father. Floresta does not discuss the role of fathers in the upbringing of children, limiting her analysis to criticism of the habit of sending young children to be cared for by villagers in a commercial arrangement by mothers who themselves had the time and the means to take responsibility for their young children's care and education. Although Floresta does not discuss the role of fathers in raising children, in *Woman* Floresta and her friend, the child's grandmother, make a practical decision to send the young child back to the father's care. In this setting, Floresta reflects upon these "repulsive customs" (Floresta 1995, p. 8) of the French, which she later characterizes as a "monstrosity" and "barbarism" in offering her views on the social role of mothers and on children's education.

While in former works Floresta's arguments are based on the equality that follows from the universality of reason, in *Woman* she offers a gendered concept of virtue as distinguishing women's proper virtues. It shows Floresta speaking to the women of her time, trying to convince them to be less egoistic and vain, by taking responsibility for themselves and their offspring. In this work, there is a defense of children's rights, a criticism of the class divide (of poor women being paid to care for the children of the French bourgeoisie), and the use of Christian morality in defense of education of the heart for women.[19] Concerned about women's modern habits and social expectations regarding children's education, Floresta takes an angry tone toward women's lack of enlightenment with respect to their own virtues. She wants to argue that despite not having access to educational institutions, and despite the social constraints that limit their autonomy, women still have political power (and a holy responsibility) as mothers.

In *Direitos*, *Lágrima*, *Opúsculo*, *Páginas*, and Woman, we see Floresta criticizing the cultural habits of modernity that promote social inequalities. She denounces injustices by claiming that the different groups that make up Brazilian society (although not all are considered to be citizens) should be treated as equals in civil society. Since they are, by nature, equals – that is, they are free rational beings with feelings and dignity – they should all contribute to the building of society, be paid for their work, and recognized in their roles. For Floresta, this is the true principle of progress of nations. Although the language and tone when talking about these various groups differs because Floresta uses popular jargon, in all cases she argues for a change in the unjust postcolonial system.

---

[19] In *Woman*, Floresta argues that women have a natural disposition to perform social functions related to care (such as educating children and being responsible for constructing a virtuous household grounded on moral principles). The development of an education that highlights these natural dispositions in women is what Floresta calls an "education of the heart."

4 Equality: From Naturally Given to a Measure of Social Justice

Floresta's feminism and critique of colonialism are grounded on the assumption that human beings are equal by nature, that is, on the idea that equality is naturally given. If human beings are equal by nature, then inequality is socially constructed for the advantage of some over others. This inequality creates suffering and prevents people from fully experiencing their own virtues and capacities, becoming mere means for the benefit of others. The grounds for this argument, the thesis that human beings must be equal by nature, appears in Floresta's first publication, *Direitos*.[20] In the *Opúsculo humanitário*, Floresta's central work, we can see how she develops the thesis first proposed in *Direitos*.

The construction of the thesis that equality is a natural fact (and therefore a natural right) appears, most prominently, in chapters two, five, and six of *Direitos*. In these chapters, Floresta, a translator who was addressing and dedicating her translation to Brazilian academics and Brazilian women, asks whether women are inferior in their ability of understanding, naturally capable of teaching the sciences, and capable of being workers.[21] In chapters three and four, she asks whether women are fit to govern and for public office.[22] Throughout the whole book, and in each chapter, the question is whether women's inferior situation and absence from public affairs is due to a natural deficiency or to unjust social norms. The argumentative strategy involves describing how male dominance over women is pervasive, extending from examples of men's lack of esteem for women to the exposition of frequently held opinions about women's alleged physical and intellectual inferiority. The targeted critique interprets common facts such as women not holding public office, not being well-educated, not being active in investigating or teaching the sciences, and not governing in states as evidence of women's weakness. Then there is a defense of natural equality with examples of women's intellectual virtues and physical abilities within the spaces they can occupy, followed by

---

[20] As *Direitos* is a Portuguese translation from the French translation of a text that was originally written in English, I will not translate Floresta's translation back into English. I am using the wording of the 1739 Sophia pamphlet, since Floresta's translation is very close to the original English.

[21] In the title of chapter 6, Floresta makes a deliberate change to the French translation that was true to the original Sophia text. In both the French translation and the original English text, the chapter is about whether women are naturally qualified for military office (this appears in chapter 7 of Sophia and in chapter 6 of the French translation). But in Floresta's translation, instead of discussing military office specifically, she treats the discussion as being about public offices in general, and the word "military" is absent from her Portuguese text; see Soares (2017).

[22] In the French text, the expression used is "si les femmes sont propres" and, in Portuguese, "se as mulheres são ou não próprias." In the original, the word "capable" indicates a natural capacity. In Portuguese and French, the vocabulary used, "próprias"/"propres" has the sense of being fit to perform a certain function.

a critique of the social habits and norms that prevent women from expressing their virtues more fully and widely.

For example, in chapter five of *Direitos*,[23] the argument offered is that if university chairs are not occupied by women, it is not because of women's lack of ability or lack of desire to fill them, but due to men's denial of their rightful access to those positions. Women should have the right to occupy university chairs because they have natural rhetorical qualities and, being more eloquent than men, they could easily put this natural virtue to good use. Women are more eloquent than men because they can persuade men of their wants and defend their rights without the help of the law. Because they are able to persuade while common opinion is against them, women must have a better rhetorical quality than men who, in their turn, need the help of law and customs to maintain their status. Since women cannot rely on social status to have their rhetorical abilities recognized, the only explanation for their linguistic virtues is that they are naturally given. So, the conclusion is that women have natural virtues and these virtues are suppressed by men, who do not allow them to be cultivated so as to maintain their position of power. This obstruction to women's flourishing is characterized as an act of violence:

> Of *Rhetoric*, we must be allow'd to be by nature design'd mistresses and models. *Eloquence* is a talent so natural and peculiar to *Woman*, that no one can dispute it her [*sic*]. *Women* can persuade what they please; and can dictate, defend, or distinguish between right and wrong, without the help of laws ... if we are endow'd with a more communicative eloquence than they are, we must be at least as well qualified as they to *teach* the *sciences*; and if we are not seen in *university chairs*, it cannot be attributed to our want of capacity to fill them, but to that violence with which the *Men* support their unjust intrusion into our places. (Sophia 1739, pp. 39–40)

The same kind of reasoning is used to demonstrate women's capacity to practice physic ("restore health to the sick and preserve it to the well") and to be female philosophers ("Might we not then by this means be both as learned *philosophers* and as able *divines* as the *Men*, as capable of being taught, and as successful in *teaching*, at least, as they are?") (Sophia 1739, p. 44). The conclusion is that if women are able to negotiate and argue for their rights while having all the odds against them, it is because of their superior talents.

Floresta's *Direitos* is, as we have seen, a translation of an anonymous English pamphlet; but as she chose to translate this particular text containing these ideas to convince Brazilian citizens of the rightful roles of women, it is safe to say that although the ideas were not originally Floresta's creation, she did hold them and

---

[23] In the 1739 Sophia pamphlet, it is chapter 6.

they impacted her. In the *Opúsculo*, Floresta reconstructs the theses from *Direitos* (chapter 27) and further elaborates on them. If, in *Direitos*, we saw the defense of women's natural rights based on the natural givenness of the equality of the sexes, in the *Opúsculo* she argues that the education of women is a measure of social justice or of civilization: "The education of women has a powerful influence on the morality of cultures and their education is the most noticeable trait of civilization in a nation" (Floresta 1989a, p. 46). As the education of women is a measure of civilizational development, in the *Opúsculo* the goal is to show not only that inequality between the sexes is socially constructed, but how various cultures approach this differences between the sexes – and how they treat women and their education – in order to reveal the mechanisms that sustain inequality. Equating civilization with social justice, Floresta suggests that the right direction of progress lies in the recognition of people's humanity and dignity.

In the *Opúsculo*, Floresta defends the education of women for the sake of their emancipation and toward the construction of social bonds based on mutual recognition of everyone's dignity. She conceives of women's participation in society as that whereby they can exercise their intellectual autonomy and be recognized as the owners of their bodies. The right approach to the female body, Floresta argues, is a consequence of women's self-understanding and self-esteem, which is shown in moderation and the absence of vanity. She opens chapter 27 by arguing that women are educated to adorn their bodies and act as if they were frail as a strategy to prevent them from having the right to education. But, metaphysically speaking, woman, Floresta says, is "like man, just as the sublime Plato says, she is a soul making use of a body" (Floresta 1989a, p. 62). She continues,

> it is an absurdity, then, a real profanation, to pretend that this soul – a work of the Creator to whom it has to return – dedicates the body that animates her swift passage through life, only to futile adornments, fake benevolence, and to please the hours of leisure to a creature that is equal to her and that we see yielding to the empire of senses more than of reason. (Floresta 1989a, p. 62).

In stimulating vanity, and using it as a strategy of domination to keep women under their unjustified power, men do not allow women to develop their rational abilities. However, Floresta says, intelligence has no sex and can be equally superior in women.

This state of affairs with respect to women's education is not limited to Brazil. A central thesis of *Opúsculo* is the idea that if we consider history through the lens of women's dignity and right to education, we see that the nations we take to be "great" or "glorious" were not civilized enough:

In Asia, this wonderful cradle of the human kind and of philosophy, women have always been considered as an instrument for the material pleasure of men or as men's most submissive slave; in this sense, their nations, even those that achieved the highest praises and glory ... remained in deep ignorance with respect to this sense of civilization that could only be transmitted to the world through the emancipation of women. (Floresta 1989a, p. 3)

The purpose of *Opúsculo* is to offer an analysis of where Brazil lies as a nation with respect to the dignity of its citizens, and to suggest significant changes in the educational methods inherited from the colonial period. At the start, Floresta analyzes various examples of Western civilized nations, citing the women that have stood out. She does not offer a list or a catalogue of women in the traditional sense, but highlights particular examples. For instance, in Portugal, she remembers Públia Hortência de Castro (1548–95) and reproduces the stories surrounding her life. Hortência de Castro wore male clothing and pretended to be a man, and she went to the University of Coimbra with her brother, becoming a prolific writer.

Having spent some time analyzing ancient, medieval, and early modern history, focusing on the role of women in different cultures that were considered to be exemplars of civilizational development, Floresta criticizes women's right to education in Brazil, denouncing general inaction:

Nothing, however, or almost nothing is being done to remove the obstacles that inhibit the progress of the education of our women, so they are able to conquer the darkness that overshadows their intelligence, so they can know the infinite sweetness of an intellectual life, a kind of life that women of any free and civilized nation should have the right to live. (Floresta 1989a, p. 44)

In the second and third parts of the *Opúsculo*, Floresta offers an explanation of the causes of the inaction and proposes educational reform in order to at least start a process of change (she is skeptical about whether every problem can be solved through education due to the limitations of people and institutions). Her explanation is grounded in a critique of tradition in the spirit of practical Cartesianism: the topic of the education of women is hard to deal with because of the strong prejudices that are sustained by individuals who consider that the opinions of their predecessors were correct. She says: "A subject that is hard and the more so as we have to face ingrained prejudices and the puzzling self-love of those who judge things as going very well just because that was the opinion of their predecessors" (Floresta 1989a, p. 45).

Floresta's radical doubt with respect to colonial values demands a revision of colonial beliefs, specifically with respect to education. She explicitly attributes to colonialism the cause of women's social situation in Brazil:

It is a sad truth that Brazil has inherited from its colonizers (*metrópole*) the neglect that they always had with the education of women. The Portuguese, carrying their guns and their campaigners to other regions of the world, exploring the glory of uniting these forces that they knew well how to employ to subjugate other nations, would get too inebriated in their great triumphs to be concerned with, as they should have, the instruction of women, who, according to the opinion of the majority of people in their country ... do not need any other knowledge besides those that make them be the first and most useful servant of their household. (Floresta 1989a, p. 47)

Floresta is aware that when she is reading the social situation of women in Brazil, she is talking about a particular group of women. She is focusing on those who "the men of this civilization consider to be Brazilian women," that is, "non-indigenous women that are born in freed-families, or those who are lucky to have their fathers rescue them, on the baptismal sink, from the sad stamp of slavery" (Floresta 1989a, p. 46). This strategy is chosen because she is writing to learned men in Brazil who have the power to change laws and public practices. That is why, to find Floresta's views on Indigenous women and black males, we have to analyze her work more broadly, including her Indigenist poem (*Lágrima* 1849) and her literary abolitionist piece (*Páginas* 1854).

Considered to be Floresta's central and most important work, the *Opúsculo humanitário* has similarities in style with *Direitos*, and the argumentative strategies employed make clear the influence of the British pamphlet on her major work. Both texts are aimed at the wider public and both use traditional logic as an instrument of persuasion, offering a charged rhetoric although differing in tone. *Opúsculo* considers the conservative stance of the Brazilian aristocracy, so the rhetoric employed sounds less radical than Sophia's. But Floresta is employing the same rationalistic strategy of explicitly using logic to convince readers.[24]

If all men, however, had a just spirit, as Helvecius thinks, would we see the great social edifice being every day threatened here and there to collapse over its most well grounded foundations? If things were this way, what would have been the goal of Aristotle, who took time to compose his Logic, so precious and so useful to the enlightenment of ideas and to the perfectibility of reason? And why would men need to study philosophy, that unfortunately so few probe and practice? (Floresta 1989a, p. 65)

Floresta claims that humans are not naturally just and have to be educated and stimulated to become so. One of the methods of education is the correct

---

[24] In a chapter on Floresta's philosophy, Secco and Pugliese (in press) develop Dorlin's (2001) thesis that Sophia and Poulain are part of the "logical feminism" movement by showing how Floresta is also part of this movement.

application of reason. Although Floresta believes, like the anonymous Sophia, that men and women have equal capacity for intelligence, she does not believe that every person (male and female) can be instructed in the same way. So she ends chapter 28 arguing that colonization makes Brazil's social situation different from that of other nations, recognizing that every woman should receive the instruction that is proper to their specific situation, while offering the means to allow them to cultivate their spirit.

In the following section, I show that Floresta generally critiques the colonial principle that operates throughout social relationships in Brazilian culture, which prevents its people from being fully developed through instruction. For Floresta, there needs to be a transformation in the colonial heritage with respect to all areas of culture, including the social situations of women, Indigenous people, and enslaved black people. This transformation in habits and, ultimately, the law, is the condition for true human progress and civilizational development.

5 The Colonialist Principle: Instrumentalization of Suffering as a Strategy of Domination

In order to better locate Floresta's arguments with respect to what needs to be transformed to construct a just society after colonization, I have mapped Floresta's description of the exploitation of Indigenous lands and the bodies of black enslaved people in the colonial context to articulate what I call "the colonialist principle." In this section, my argument is that Floresta shows the ways in which this principle works in Brazil – a colonial society that needs to overcome its former colonial status in order to become a truly independent nation. These themes are present in Floresta's *A lágrima de um caeté* (1849) and *Páginas de uma vida obscura* (1854). Through an analysis of these literary works, I explain what Floresta meant by colonialism and its principles of operation.

From the viewpornt of nineteenth-century Brazilian society, an empire employing slave labor and expanding its dominion through the expropriation of Indigenous lands, Floresta conceives colonialism as a mechanism that instrumentalizes the suffering of others. According to Floresta, black enslaved peoples, Indigenous peoples, and Brazilian women are all subject to arbitrary tyrannical authority at different levels. They are treated as less than human and their capacity for self-affirmation is unjustly limited. Although she is pessimistic about whether a real transformation is possible, Floresta suggests that colonialist education could be overcome by means of a change in institutions (e.g. abolition of slavery), political practices, and educational practice. Through literary descriptive strategies, she displays the structures of colonialism as the practice of intentionally causing suffering to others as a political strategy.

In the *Opúsculo humanitário*, Floresta argues that the way a nation treats the education of its women is indicative of their degree of civilizational develop-ment. If a nation's citizens do not treat their own women – who inhabit their households and are mothers of their children – with dignity, it is more likely that they will not treat other people with dignity. Hence, the condition of women's education is a measure of social justice. Floresta argues that the lack of interest in women's education in nineteenth-century Brazil is the result of former colonial practices that have been inherited.

Although Floresta was herself the owner of a school for girls and acted as school director, promoting a progressive curriculum, when she talks about education in the *Opúsculo humanitário*, she does not limit her analysis to institutions and the explicit curricula they follow. Instead, she thinks of educa-tion as encompassing what is learned through interaction with others in the social environment. Floresta argues that as long as there are people suffering for the sake of sustaining the privilege of a few at the expense of the life and dignity of others, and as long as there are people in the nation who are intentionally being treated as if they were less than human, the educational experience of every citizen of the nation will be negatively impacted by these existing oppressions. That is, if culture and social status depend upon using others as instruments, forcing them to suffer, the social environment will not be at all fertile for human flourishing. She argues that even those who consider them-selves protected from violent spaces or situations, which are frequent in the social sphere, suffer limitations because of the lack of an environment that is broadly conducive to their development. Consequently, although some suffer more than others, every educational experience in this situation is a learning process that happens through suffering. As the goal of education is to offer opportunities for people to become virtuous citizens and act virtuously in all situations, and to experience life in its fullest form, it cannot achieve this goal if the unjust laws of colonial times are still in place.

The central mechanism that should be dismantled is using others as instruments and forcing them to act by causing them pain, a colonialist principle that is operative in various kinds of social relations. The marginal social status of groups that suffer violence results from the fact that there are people who benefit from the lack of recognition of their dignity, and continue to cause mental and physical pain. The moral lessons that the colonized are taught are just as hard and painful to unlearn as they are to learn, so they become ingrained in the culture.

Causing suffering as a strategy of domination is a colonialist principle that grounds the social mechanisms of slavery and the expropriation of lands.

In *Lágrima* and *Páginas*, the relationship between the colonialist strategy and the situation of Indigenous peoples and the black population is exposed. In *Lágrima*, Floresta describes the native *caetés* (an Indigenous nation) as off-springs of nature, descendants who have a natural right to their lands. As they naturally belong to their forests, they are the rightful owners. Throughout the poem, Floresta narrates their transition from being protagonists of their own histories to becoming spectators of those very same stories. According to Duarte:

> far from mystifying her character, she builds him from concrete data coming from Brazilian reality. The evidence for this lies in the fact that her hero is a defeated indigenous man. From since the beginning [of the poem], defeated. While in other writings [of the time] one can more easily find the image of the indigenous that fights ("brave and strong") and that sometimes wins, in Nísia we have the native already defeated and, what is most important, conscious of his own defeat. For this reason, from being the main character of the Brazilian story he comes to be depicted as a mere spectator, as he lies in the margins of the historical process, with the position of the observer of the new emerging battles as the only thing that is left for him (Duarte 1999, p. 167).

Duarte shows that Floresta constructs a different image of Brazilian Indigenous peoples. The prevailing view, which influenced the European imaginary in the concept of the savage (Montaigne, Locke, and Rousseau, for example) is of an Indigenous person who is naturally good and kind (Franco 1976).

The first half of *A lágrima de um caeté* contains a description of Indigenous peoples' land as well as their bodies, resulting in the annihilation of their culture and the destruction of their dignity:

> To the domination of oppressive tyrants, That in name of the pious heaven came
> To take the possessions that heaven bestowed on us
> Our wives, our daughter, our peace have stolen from us!
> . . .
> Bringing from across the ocean the laws, the vices,
> putting away our laws and our traditions! (Floresta 2021a, p. 17)

As a suffering body that listens, hopelessly, to his own story of loss, the *caeté* is pictured as someone who is conscious of his defeat (Duarte, 1999, p. 163). Floresta shows that his lack of hope is a consequence of constant repression. By being constantly subjugated, the Indigenous man has learned the lesson of the colonizer and has internalized his own sorrow and sadness. The poem has the tone of an elegy and "is structured around the duality of oppressed/oppressor, colonized/colonizer, indigenous/white, savage/ civilized" (Duarte, 1999, p. 160). By internalizing the condition of conquered and defeated, the native *caeté* become completely dominated for they identify themselves with defeat.

Floresta is careful to show that this identification is the result of a social construction, an act of violence, and not the result of the natural, biological condition of Indigenous people. The same is true for black enslaved people. At the time, scientific racism and biological theories that defended the inferiority of races were very common. Floresta systematically distances herself from these theories, arguing that no race is better than any other; everyone is, by nature, equal.

In *Lágrima*, the colonizers are described as having used Indigenous suffering as an instrument of discipline and control, stealing not only Indigenous lands but also the people's dignity. The situation is pictured as a cultural and economic problem, but also as a moral issue leading to loss of culture, loss of agency, and the loss of one's sense of belonging. The *caeté*, nevertheless, rebels against the injustice and fights in the Praieira Revolt, protesting against the colonizers together with other liberals. In the poem, Floresta describes this popular revolt, which actually took place in the northeast of Brazil, but she focuses on the Indigenous men who are participants in the defeated popular movement. Although Floresta limits her analysis to Indigenous men in *Lágrima*, in the final chapters of the *Opúsculo* she focuses on Indigenous women, who she describes as symbols of strength. They are praised for being workers, good mothers, and as female figures who recognize the importance of nurturing interpersonal relations (Floresta 1989a, p. 147). Floresta cannot hide her grief when she says that Indigenous women were the first to suffer the violence of colonizers.

The colonialist principle of using someone else's suffering for one's own benefit is clearly present across all dimensions of the institution of slavery, in which the indifference to the pain of another becomes the condition for many kinds of gain in the colonial economy. At the core of the economic system is the subjugation and dehumanization of black enslaved people. In *Páginas de uma vida obscura*, Floresta depicts scenes of suffering and domination. While undergoing various sacrifices, the male slave Domingos is not recognized for his moral deeds and is never rewarded. *Páginas* is a narrative that depicts the sorrows of black men who are upright and morally good, but who are always used by others, not only for their physical strength but also their moral fortitude. Floresta's critique of slavery is also present in the *Opúsculo*, where she claims that constant psychological humiliation and physical punishment turns the black enslaved into automatons: they are treated as if they were "pack animals" or "machines whose springs should move according to the wills and fancies of their owners" (Floresta 1989a, p. 116). They are denied freedom of thought, are oppressed by work, and they become "souls on a carcass," so they have no choice other than to suffer in silence with no defense other than their own tears, no warranty other than blind obedience, no vengeance other than their mute prayer to God:

> God who no race made
> To have over another
> revolting superiority,
> unlimited pleasure. (Floresta 1989a, p. 116)

The verse that Floresta cites as the prayer of the slave also appears in *Lágrima de um caeté* as the prayer of the Indigenous *caeté*. The fact that enslaved and Indigenous people both pray the same verse highlights the proximity of their social situations and circumstances as the colonized. Floresta describes them as sorrowful races that have to learn "pernicious lessons," being "condemned to the education by the whip," and becoming "demoralized by the captivity" (Floresta 1989a, p. 96). Disciplined by suffering, the dehumanization of the black population was the result of the social practice of forced labor.[25] In a later work, *Trois ans en Italie* (1864), Floresta is explicit when, in defense of abolition, she addresses the citizens of Brazil: "Break, oh! break the shackles of your slaves!" (Floresta 1998b, p. 41).

Floresta argues that this "education by the whip" is reflected in various levels of the culture, even in "Brazilian women" who are not slaves. As shown in Section I, Floresta employs the same language of "slavery" that Sophia used in her pamphlet. Recognizing the tyrannical authority that men exercise over women, she sees the situation of Brazilian women as analogous to that of slaves. However, the only time Floresta calls Brazilian women slaves is when she is reconstructing the arguments from *Direitos* in the *Opúsculo*. All other occurrences of the term "slave" that appear in *Opúsculo* refer to enslaved people who were not considered to be citizens, showing that Floresta is attentive to social historical differences. Brazilian women who are not slaves, in this context, are mostly slave owners. Hence, Floresta calls these women "patrícias" indicating their noble status and privilege among the group of women that form Brazilian society.

With respect to women, specifically, the structure of domination Floresta identifies is the same as that which had formerly been expressed in *Direitos*, the translation of the Sophia pamphlet. Women are educated to see themselves as frail and weak, so that men have a reason to keep them under their care.

---

[25] Beatriz Nascimento, a Brazilian historian, shows that black Brazilians resignified their sufferings into various forms of resistance; she argues that the myth of the resilient and obedient slave was a cultural construction to prevent black Brazilians from constructing a stronger self-identity based on the examples of powerful black leaders (Nascimento 1985). Nascimento shows that the concept of "quilombos" is important in reconstructing black Brazilian history from the point of view of the peoples' virtues and deeds. "Quilombos" is the name given to self-governed black communities in Brazil, similar to the maroon communities in the Caribbean.

However, since all women are potential mothers, they have the innate capacity and duty to be the primary caregivers of men, and of every citizen. Nevertheless, this caregiving role is not socially recognized when it is performed by women, but only when it is practiced by men in order to control their women. Hence, there is injustice in the way that the labor of care is valued. Floresta also criticizes Rousseau and the idea that women should be educated to please men (Floresta 1989a, p. 27). When Rousseau "counsels women to have taste for adornments (which he considers to be natural in women) and embellish the gifts of the body by using their physical beauty and artifice to subjugate men," he is "considering the woman only from the material point of view and doing nothing but taking away all the dignity of her nature" (Floresta 1989a, p. 61).[26] Floresta argues that this kind of education results in teaching women vices such as lust and vanity, preventing them from knowing themselves as a soul–body complex that is able to learn and live virtuously, just like men. Floresta sees this kind of education for women as a way of contributing to "increasing the number, already considerably high, of [women] slaves" (Floresta 1989a, p. 62), since it maintains and increases their dependence.

In the essay *Woman*, Floresta uses a more radical tone in an attempt to call women's attention to their potential and capacities by elevating the tasks they are usually expected to perform as women to a political level. An appeal to Catholic values is also used to reverse another vice associated with noble women's education: egotism resulting from idleness and vanity. As Floresta's major concern is the education of women, all other criticisms she offers of colonial society are part of a larger project of understanding the specific causes that limit the learning and expression of virtues and the development of nations. She starts from the principle that there are no differences among the sexes and races, and everyone should be treated as equals. The immediate consequence of this is condemnation of colonization as a practice that unjustly creates a sense of superiority of some over others by means of violence. She then generalizes the effects of violence, showing that it not only has harmful effects on the individuals who are the focus of the oppression, but becomes ingrained in social habits, creating a noxious cultural environment.

Floresta has two major points to make: first, that education happens inside educational institutions but, most importantly, outside of them as well; for this reason, as long as there is a violent environment, education – even in protected spaces, even in selected schools, even of the elite – will be affected by violence and will reproduce violence. So, as long as we live under colonial principles, no

---

[26] Floresta attributes the thesis not only to Rousseau but also to Olinthus Gilbert Gregory (1774–1841), an English mathematician who was the founder of the Royal Astronomical Society.

one will fully flourish. Second, the immediate issue for the education of women (her major topic of concern, although this point can be applied to the education of men and women alike) is that teaching should not be an act of domination: schools should not reproduce the culture of violence of colonial society in any way. The most important point is to unlearn colonial education, and to construct a social environment in which everyone is treated with dignity and as equals. As a consequence, Floresta rejects all kinds of corporal punishment as a means of discipline and defends an education that nourishes the intellect, protects the body from pain, and promotes social justice.

6 Dignity as True Liberation: Educating for Physical and Intellectual Emancipation

Underlying Floresta's philosophy of education is her positive suggestion to counteract the lessons of colonialism, untangle its cultural consequences, and provide the conditions for a full expression of civil equality. As we have seen, the condition of the education of women is a measure of social justice in any society. Floresta argued that the lack of interest in women's education in nineteenth-century Brazil was the result of colonial practices. In this section, I present Floresta's argument on the role of the body in the acquisition of true liberation. Floresta brings the role of the body into the picture because she is reflecting upon the physical punishment of slaves, Indigenous peoples, and the various kinds of violence suffered by women. For her, education should restore the dignity of individuals by nourishing their minds while protecting their bodies from unnecessary pain.

In the *Opúsculo*, Floresta claims that since "woman is, like man, as said Plato, a soul making use of a body" (Floresta 1989a, p. 62), it is absurd to neglect and misuse the body. She defends women's right to scientific education, arguing that cultivation through books has a role in giving meaning to one's life. Women should cultivate their intellect so as not to live without purpose, and lacking knowledge of themselves and their role. Associated with intellectual cultivation, there should be a healthy relationship with the body so that a sense of moral dignity can be built. It is only when body and mind are taken care of that individuals can discover their social roles and occupy a social space that fulfills their potential and that of the community. Floresta calls attention to the role of the body in the acquisition of true liberation, showing that a free and healthy body is necessary, not only for full intellectual development, but also for the construction of a social organization that is conducive to everyone's flourishing. The implication of her philosophy of education, then, is that suffering does not dignify – dignity lies in physical and intellectual emancipation.

This idea that true liberation only happens with physical and intellectual emancipation is a thesis that connects Floresta's defense of women's right to education and her specific claims on teaching practices. As an early postcolonial thinker of the nineteenth century, Floresta is interested in mapping the theoretical and political structures of colonialism that prevent the development of nations, especially Brazil. By analyzing the violent social practices involving black enslaved people and Indigenous people, she describes physical and psychological punishments as broadly employed colonial disciplinary and educational strategies. As a correctional technique, violence is employed so as to turn an action into an example that should not be repeated. Floresta locates the origins of these disciplinary strategies in the inquisitorial practices of torture during the Holy Office tribunals that "under another form and with a different end, traveled through the Atlantic, orienting the education of Brazilian children, conducted by severe jesuits or charlatan instructors" (Floresta 1989a, p. 58). This education through violence was not limited to formal institutes of education but was pervasive in Brazilian homes, where parents educated their children using a rigor that "was not less cruel" (Floresta 1989a, p. 58). Floresta shows that the various kinds of reproduction of violence within Brazilian society are the result of colonialism and the institution of slavery.

She describes educational institutions of the time as follows: "Early childhood educational institutions used to have the appearance of prisons rather than of an educational space. The method of hand-paddling (*palmatória*) and of cane was usually adopted as the best incentive for the development of intelligence" (Floresta 1989a, p. 57). Even if girls were spared the physical violence, they were not exempt from witnessing it and receiving all sorts of verbal punishments. In chapter 46 of *Opúsculo*, Floresta describes how vanity as a moral vice can cause physical harm when she narrates the tragic case of a girl in a corset who was a student at Floresta's own school.[27] The case is the story of a little girl of just six years of age who was very kind and loved by everyone. Every day that she would come to class and the director of the school would see her breathe with difficulty, so she would come over to her and unfasten her corset. Observing the child's routine and the recurrence of her breathing difficulties, the director talked to the mother to ask her to reconsider the use of the corset as it was dangerously compressing her lungs. The director explains to the mother that children need to "move freely to well develop" (Floresta 1989a, p. 106), but the mother ignored the school director, considering that keeping the child well-dressed was more important. The child went to the theater and the mother

---

[27] According to Peggy-Sharpe (Floresta 1989a, p. 106, n. 161), Floresta was describing a case she witnessed.

constantly flattered her on how beautiful she looked in her clothes. On the following day, when she was being prepared to go to school, the little girl allowed the mother to tighten the corset even more. As soon as she entered the classroom, the director saw the girl lose her breath, faint, and die.

This tragic scene illustrates how the body is used as an artifice for social recognition, but also how inflicting and suffering pain is an accepted practice for the sake of social status. Floresta characterizes "the sad and revolting spectacle, for having been caused by the pretension of a mother to turn her daughter [into] someone distinguished by her body" (Floresta 1989a, p. 106). This is another sense in which a social life based on instrumentalization of suffering reproduces violence. That is the reason why, together with the abolition of slavery, there is a need for collective liberation from colonial principles. Floresta offers all kinds of examples of the propagation of violence in the home. She talks about girls who learned to subjugate their wet nurses by seeing the way their parents treated the women slaves. She refers to this "revolting ingratitude" (Floresta 1989a, p. 96) as a "pernicious example" that these girls will pass on to their own children. Floresta describes various domestic scenes, arguing that as long as there is slavery, violence will be repeated continuously and a complete education will not be fully fulfilled.

From these cases, Floresta goes on to distinguish education as illustration and education as a form of moral dignity, a practice that can never be successful through violent strategies. For Floresta, the suffering of students should not be instrumentalized to make them learn. The acquisition of knowledge and the expression of virtues should be liberatory experiences. Hence, educational institutions should aid the construction of free, healthy, liberated bodies, which can never be achieved by torturing a person (either physically or psychologically). Social pressures due to a wrong view of the role of the body cause distress about physical appearance. These pressures can lead to physical and emotional problems because they nurture a sense of inferiority, weakness, and incapacity. Floresta argues that the common-sensical view that women should show frailty in order to be beautiful and desired is another mechanism of humiliation and subjugation. Again, this kind of instrumentalization of the suffering of girls indicates the need for their complete emancipation: from a sense of physical and intellectual inferiority to the construction of an identity that overcomes these violent lessons.

Floresta argues that women's physical or material emancipation is as important, in every dimension, as their intellectual freedom. She argues that women should be freed from the constraints of garments that cause physical pain and have the potential to do further harm. She also argues that women should be freed from the limitations of the household space, which prevents them from occupying public spaces that are regarded as exclusively male (such as the university or the workforce more generally). Interestingly, Floresta does not think that childbearing and breastfeeding constitute physical constraints. As women have a natural potential to bear children, she claims that the capacity to give birth and nourish is a strength, a physical virtue. She argues that women should want to breastfeed and nourish their newborns, thus rejecting the prevailing view that black enslaved women should act as wet nurses for white women and that black women should not breastfeed their own children.

Finally, it is also a matter of women's physical and material emancipation that they should be allowed to hold public office. If they are dependent on men to decide legal affairs that directly impact their well-being, this has material implications for their whole life. Intellectual emancipation without material emancipation is, in this way, useless, because women will be able to decide what is best for them and for others and will not be able to act accordingly. Floresta argued that it is pointless for a family to undertake to educate their children well if the habits of the nation remain violent. As long as there is slavery, as long as people live under colonial principles, no one can be educated to their full potential. She appeals to the role of reform in both public and private spheres, and to an education that teaches that everybody is equal and deserving of dignity and moral recognition. As women are body–soul complexes, their education should not be limited to intellectual development, but should also embrace understanding of their own bodies. This includes figuring out one's own social role and function, so women are able to work and to serve society beyond the limits of the household. For Floresta, women should become thinking beings in healthy bodies within a just society.

In this section, I examined the practical arguments concerning the operationalization of the colonialist principle in Floresta's critique of the social situation of women, enslaved persons, and Indigenous peoples in early postcolonial Brazil. Underlying Floresta's thinking on education is a view of modern history and the modern history of philosophy as a period marked by colonialism. The problems of colonization and its effects on all aspects of life were unavoidable. However, recovering authors from the colonial and early postcolonial period is no easy task, for it involves untangling the philosophical theses that were written at a time when the complex structures of colonization were still in place. But, given that the effects of colonialism can be felt even today, this analysis can shed light on the hidden social norms that are still carried unreflectively.

7 Locating Floresta in the History of Philosophy

I now conclude with some reflections on the place of Floresta in the traditional philosophical canon. Traditional narratives on early modern and modern philosophy center around the events of the scientific revolution, the political crises of the time, and the Protestant Reformation (Popkin 1979). In retrieving the works of Floresta, however, there has to be some further addition to the historically relevant events, to reinforce the narrative that the discovery of the New World was one of the key causes of the philosophical skepticism of modernity. Moreover, Floresta's work contributes to the historical context by bringing a different vocabulary and a new set of arguments and questions. With respect to vocabulary, she does not speak, as Montaigne does, for example, in his essay *On Cannibals*, of discovery of the New World. She uses the language of "tyrannical oppressors," of "ambitious" colonizers who "cause suffering by barbarian means" and committed a "nefarious and terrible crime" having "stolen" the lands, the wives, and the culture of the Indigenous population (Floresta 2021a, p. 16). Her works highlight the importance of taking colonialism and its economic machinery – the institution of slavery – as central to the emergence of modern thought.

With respect to the new set of arguments and questions Floresta raises, they all involve historically informed philosophical reflection, both on the social situation of the various groups that make up Brazilian identity (she is concerned with matters of gender and race) and on the power dynamics between Brazil and Europe, in order to criticize so-called civilized habits (of modern France, most especially, since she lived there for many decades toward the end of her life). By using the notion of natural equality to argue for women's rights, and by expanding its consequences beyond a feminist agenda, Floresta should be read as a practical Cartesian philosopher who puts the application of Cartesianism to the test by defending the dignity of enslaved persons and the Indigenous populations. She also sheds new light on the social role of women by reframing the political meaning of the household and of childbearing. Controversial from today's perspective, Floresta offers a defense of women's role as mothers, wives, and daughters as a way "to preserve dignity in submission and authority in obedience" (Floresta 1865, p. 25). Floresta's defense of women's political role in the household is not an argument in favor of limiting their role to the household. As a public philosopher, she was interested in reaching the common women who were living under patriarchal authority inside their private homes, and educated to be submissive and to cultivate vanity to please men. In her works on the moral education of women, Floresta argues that even under such conditions women can have political power and exercise their intellectual freedom. She claims that women can subvert cultural customs at the same time as they fulfill cultural expectations. The argument seems paradoxical, however: Floresta claims that it is possible to exercise self-denial as a form of freedom.

In her moral works, *Woman* being a particularly important example, Floresta is highlighting the fact that mothers are the educators of future citizens. The call for responsibility is based on her observations of ingrained social habits, such as transferring the care of children and the household to wet nurses and slaves (in France, care was transferred to poor women and children). Affluent women, according to Floresta, have too much time that is badly employed. Wealthy women's lack of political responsibility is a problem that she confronts using childbearing and traditional values as instruments of persuasion. Moreover, as she was a Catholic, and understood the role of religion in shaping society, Floresta appealed to religious virtues in a call for action. Affluent women should not live a life of idleness using their time to entertain men, host events, and exclusively care about their physical appearance. Instead, they should cultivate virtues such as abnegation so that they could become less egoistic and more inclined to hold themselves accountable for their social roles as caregivers, role models, and educators. One issue that Floresta considers to be very important in moral education is that affluent women, understanding the power and potency of their own female bodies, should take responsibility for nurturing their offspring by breastfeeding them.

This critique of the habits of the time can be hard to untangle for a contemporary audience that is familiar with the concept of a caring mother (Margutti, 2019, p. 60) and has witnessed new configurations of family structures, household gender roles, and parental accountability. The critique that Floresta places an unfair burden on women and offers a conservative feminism (Matthews, 2012, p. 68) is not unfounded. Such a critique, however, is anachronistic and lacks the contextual subtlety that is brought to the surface when we analyze the cultural habits of different groups of women, especially those from varying social and historical circumstances. Floresta speaks to women of a particular social class and economic background and, in doing so, she opens space for every woman – including enslaved black women who did not have the right – to be able to nurture, breastfeed, and care for their own offspring. She points out that Indigenous women are to be praised for the way they connect their children with the life of the village and with their own work, and she takes them as exemplars of virtuous females.

In this way, Floresta offers a critique of modernity and defends women's right to full development as human beings while maintaining a tragic sense of acceptance of women's current social situation. She argues that even when there is no chance to learn in an institutional setting, and even when there is no opportunity to occupy public office, there is still dignity and freedom in being a woman. The proposed solution is to assume the private role and use it politically as a transformative force on social habits, by becoming exemplars and developing proper female virtues. In all her works on the moral education of women, Floresta makes the background assumption that men and women are metaphysical equals in terms of the nature of their intellects. Given women's upbringing as future mothers and wives, that is, they have been trained and are expected to be generous and assume caregiving roles, Floresta argues that the result is women's moral superiority compared with men. Acknowledging traditional gendered expectations, she considers that these socially constructed differences lead to a distinct set of virtues that are properly female. Recognizing women's suffering and pain, as well as the noxious effects of the neglect of the education of their intellect, Floresta defends female virtues as if they were heroic virtues that could help prevent child neglect and marital violence.

Floresta's agenda was different from those with whom she is usually associated. Although the spurious character of her translation distances Floresta from Wollstonecraft, locating her work in a much earlier feminist tradition, she is still part of the reception history of British feminism. It is important, however, to see Floresta as someone who offers a perspective that is distinct from her European contemporaries with respect to discussions on the philosophical foundations of women's rights. Born and raised in a colony, encountering many kinds of social relations that were never part of the European experience, Floresta's feminism opens a new page in the history of the *querelle des femmes*. The tensions of having the "other" within, a trait of colonial culture, are present in her writings and she is continually negotiating the conflicting heritage of European tradition and nascent Brazilian culture. Considering the influence that the anonymous Sophia pamphlet had on her works, Floresta also contributes to the discussion on social Cartesianism. Slavery and colonialism are challenges to the Cartesian principle of natural equality, and Floresta's view of the mind–body relation that underlies her defense of a feminist and anti-colonial education is a critique of theoretical Cartesianism. Starting with Cartesian principles, she puts their application to the test, making use of doctrines from the European Enlightenment to criticize this very tradition. Thinking from within, she questions the conceptual pair of barbarism and civilization (and the very existence of a true Enlightenment era), showing that those who consider themselves to be civilized (the Europeans) act with barbarism as colonizers.

Floresta was, in many ways, a pioneer,[28] but she was not the only woman of her time and context who was concerned about women's social situation and who published on women's rights. Floresta was part of a literary–philosophical

---

[28] Ximenes (2019, p. 16) argues that Floresta was Brazil's first feminist (he does not offer a reason for this description, but it is probably because of *Direitos*), the first Brazilian woman to propose and implement an educational model in the country (*Fany ou o Modelo das Donzelas*, 1847), the first Brazilian woman to write and try to publish a complete romance (*Dedicação de uma Amiga*, 1850), the first Brazilian woman to publish a book in a foreign language (*Itinéraire d'un voyage en Allemagne*, 1857), the first Brazilian writer to publish a historical fiction on slavery (*Páginas de uma vida obscura*, 1855), and the most illustrious Brazilian woman of her time.

movement in nineteenth-century Brazil, headed by women intellectuals who published in the Brazilian press. There were women writers (for example, Ana Eurídice Eufrosina de Barandas, Maria Firmina dos Reis, Josefina Álvares de Azevedo, Emília de Freitas), as well as journal editors (such as the Argentinian born but naturalized Brazilian, Juana Paula Manso), who used the press to expose, in many kinds of literary forms, the philosophical foundations of women's rights by offering powerful critiques of exclusionary European Enlightenment ideas. This intellectual circle, constituted by women thinkers, gave traction to the issue of women right's in Brazilian society long before the suffragist movement. The work of the women in this intellectual circle, based in Rio de Janeiro, was foundational to the political ideas and the moral debates of the soon-to-be-born Brazilian Republic. Floresta's translation of the Sophia pamphlet was, however, an adhesive that helped to strengthen the narratives that women were creating about themselves, and it became a foundational text in the construction of Brazilian identity. The philosophical reflections and the critical developments of those ideas in Floresta's own works remain fundamental to understanding the philosophical productions by women in Brazil, in Latin America, and in the Enlightenment beyond their national – European – tendencies.

References

Nísia Floresta's Works

Floresta, N. (1832) *Direitos das mulheres e injustiça dos homens*. Recife: Typographia Fidedigma, 1832.

(1833) *Direitos das mulheres e injustiça dos homens*. 2nd ed. Porto Alegre: Typographia de V. F. Andrade.

(1839) *Direitos das mulheres e injustiça dos homens*. 3rd ed. Rio de Janeiro [publisher unknown].

(1842) *Conselhos à minha filha*. Rio de Janeiro: Typographia de J. S. Cabral.

(1845) *Conselhos à minha filha, com 40 pensamentos em versos*. 2nd ed. Rio de Janeiro: Typographia de F. de Paula Brito.

(1847a) *Daciz ou a jovem completa: Historieta oferecida a suas educandas*. Rio de Janeiro: Typographia de F. Paula Brito.

(1847b) *Discurso que às suas educandas dirigiu Nísia Floresta* (December 18). Rio de Janeiro: Typographia Imparcial de F. Paula Brito.

(1847c) *Fany ou o modelo das donzelas*. Rio de Janeiro: Edição do Colégio Augusto.

(1849a) *A lágrima de um caeté*. Rio de Janeiro: Typographia de L. A. F. Menezes.

(1849b) *A lágrima de um caeté*. 2nd ed. Rio de Janeiro: Typographia de L. A. F. Menezes .

(1850) *Dedicação de uma amiga*, 2 vols. Niterói: Typographia Fluminense de Lopes & Cia.

(1853) *Opúsculo humanitário*. Rio de Janeiro: Typographia de M. A. Silva Lima. http://objdigital.bn.br/objdigital2/acervo_digital/div_obrasgerais/drg376981/drg376981.pdf.

(1854) *Páginas de uma vida obscura: Um passeio ao Aqueduto da Carioca: O pranto filial*. Rio de Janeiro: Typographia N. Lobo Vianna.

(1855a) Páginas de uma vida obscura. *O Brasil Ilustrado*, Rio de Janeiro, January–June. http://memoria.bn.br/DocReader/Hotpage/HotpageBN .aspx?bib=706817&pagfis=8&url=http://memoria.bn.br/docreader#.

(1855b) Passeio ao Aqueduto da Carioca. *O Brasil Ilustrado*, Rio de Janeiro, July 15, 68–70.

(1855c) Um improviso, na manhã de 1° do corrente, ao distinto literato e grande poeta António Feliciano de Castilho. *O Brasil Ilustrado*, Rio de Janeiro, April 30, 157.

(1856) O pranto filial. *O Brasil Ilustrado*, Rio de Janeiro, March 31, 141–142.

(1857) *Itineraire d'un voyage en Allemagne*. Paris: Firmin Diderot Frères et Cie.

(1858) *Consigli a mia figlia*. Florence: Stamperia Sulle Logge del Grano.

(1859a) *Conseils a ma fille*. Translated from the Italian by B. D. B. Florence: Le Monnier.

(1859b) *Consigli a mia figlia*. 2nd ed. Mandovi [publisher unknown].

(1859c) *Scintille d'un'anima brasiliana*. Florence: Tipografia Barbera, Bianchi & C.

(1860) *Le lagrime d'un caeté* (trans. E. Marcucci). Florence: Le Monnier.

(1864) *Trois ans en Italie, suivis d'un voyage en Grèce*, vol. 1. Paris: Libraire E. Dentu.

(1865) *Woman*. (trans. L. A. De Faria). London: G. Parker.

(1867) *Parsis*. Paris [publisher unknown].

(1871) *Le Brésil*. Paris: Libraire André Sagnier.

(1872) *Trois ans en Italie, suivis d'un voyage en Grèce*, vol. 2. Paris: E. Dentu Libraire-Éditeur et Jeffes.

(1878) *Fragments d'un ouvrage inédit: Notes biographiques*. Paris: A. Chérié Editeur.

Posthumous Editions

Floresta, N. (1888a) *Sete cartas inéditas de Auguste Comte a Nísia Floresta*. Rio de Janeiro: Centro do Apostolado do Brasil.

(1888b) *Sept Lettres Inédites d'Auguste Comte a Mme. Nisia Brasileira*. Rio de Janeiro: Apostolat Positiviste du Brésil.

(1903) *Cartas de Auguste Comte a Nísia Floresta* (original text and translation). *A República*, Natal, January–February.

(1929) *Auguste Comte et mme. Nísia Brasileira: Correspondance*. Paris: Libraire Albert Blanchard.

(1935) *Fanny ou o modelo das donzelas*. In Fernando Osório (ed.), *Mulheres farroupilhas*. Porto Alegre: Globo.

(1938) *A lágrima de um caeté* (foreword M. de Abreu). *Revista das Academias de Letras*, Rio de Janeiro, January.

(1982) *Itinerário de uma viagem à Alemanha* (trans. F. das Chagas Pereira). Natal: Ed. UFRN.

(1989a) *Opúsculo humanitário*. 2nd ed. (introduction and notes P. Sharpe Valladares; afterword C. Lima Duarte). São Paulo: Cortez.

(1989b) *Direitos das mulheres e injustiça dos homens*. 4th ed. (foreword, notes, and afterword C. Lima Duarte). São Paulo: Cortez.

(1995) Woman. Appendix with notes by P. Sharpe. In P. Sharpe, Nísia Floresta: "Woman" (including Livia A. de Faria's English translation of Floresta's essay). *BRASIL/BRAZIL: A Journal of Brazilian Literature*, 83–120. Brown Digital Repository, Brown University Library. https://doi .org/10.26300/847a-p309.

(1997a) *A lágrima de um caeté* (commentary and notes C. Lima Duarte). Natal: Fundação José Augusto.

(1997b) *Cintilações de uma alma brasileira* (trans. M. Vartulli; foreword and notes C. Lima Duarte). Florianópolis: Mulheres; Santa Cruz do Sul: Edunisc.

(1998a) *Itinerário de uma viagem à Alemanha*. 2nd ed. (trans. F. das Chagas Pereira; notes and commentary C. Lima Duarte). Florianópolis: Mulheres; Santa Cruz do Sul: Edunisc.

(1998b) *Três anos na Itália*, vol. I. (trans. F. das Chagas Pereira; foreword C. Lima Duarte). Natal: Ed. UFRN.

(2001) *Fragmentos de uma obra inédita: Notas biográficas* (trans. N. Bernardo da Câmara; foreword C. Lima Duarte). Brasília: Editora Universidade de Brasília.

(2002) *Cartas de Nísia Floresta & Auguste Comte* (trans. M. Lemos and P. Berinson; ed. with notes C. Lima Duarte). Florianópolis: Mulheres; Santa Cruz do Sul: Edunisc.

(2019) *Cinco obras completas* (ed. S. Barcelos Ximenes). E-book.

(2021a) *A lágrima de um caeté* (afterword and notes C. Lima Duarte). Mossoró: Sarau das Letras Editora.

(2021b) *Direitos das mulheres e injustiça dos homens* (notes and commentary C. Lima Duarte). Rio Grande do Norte: Sertão das Letras Editora.

(2021c) *Opúsculo humanitário* (ed. with foreword and commentaries C. Lima Duarte). São Paulo: Editora Blimunda.

Secondary Sources

Anonymous. (1872) Nísia Floresta. *O Novo Mundo: Periodico Illustrado do Progresso da Edade*. New York, May 23, 133. http://memoria.bn.br/docrea der/cache/5071008146871/I0000313-2-0-002271-001513-006399-004263 .JPG.

Botting, E. H. (2012) Wollstonecraft in Europe: A Revisionist Reception History, 1792–1904 (June 23, 2012). *History of European Ideas* (October). https://ssrn.com/abstract=2089864.

(2020) Nineteenth-Century Critical Reception. In N. Johnson & P. Keen (eds.), *Mary Wollstonecraft in Context* (pp. 50–56). Cambridge: Cambridge University Press. https://doi.org/10.1017/9781108261067.

Botting, E. H. & Cronin, M. (2014) A Vindication of the Rights of Woman within the Women's Human Rights Tradition, 1739–2015. In M. Wollstonecraft, *A Vindication of the Rights of Woman*, E. H. Botting (ed.). New Haven, CT: Yale University Press.

Botting, E. H. & Matthews, C. H. (2014) Overthrowing the Floresta–Wollstonecraft Myth for Latin American Feminism. *Gender & History*, 26 (1), 64–83.

Bour, I. (2022) Who Translated into French and Annotated Mary Wollstonecraft's *Vindication of the Rights of Woman? History of European Ideas*, 48(7), 879–891. https://doi.org/10.1080/01916599.2021.2022081.

Brasil. (1827) *Diario da Camara dos Senadores do Imperio do Brasil (RJ)*, 52 (1), 533 (discourses from Viscount of Cayru and Marquis of Santo Amaro). http://memoria.bn.br/DocReader/docreader.aspx?bib=709468&pasta=ano% 20182&pesq&pagfis=1161.

Broad, J. (2019) The Early Modern Period: Dignity and the Foundation of Women's Rights. In S. Bergès, E. Hunt Botting, & A. Coffee (eds.), *The Wollstonecraftian Mind*, 1st ed. (pp. 25–35). London: Routledge. https://doi .org/10.4324/9781315186788-3.

(2022) From Nobility and Excellence to Generosity and Rights: Sophia's Defenses of Women (1739–40). *Hypatia*, 37(1), 43–59. https://doi.org/10 .1017/hyp.2021.71.

Câmara, A. da (1938) A Lágrima de um Caeté. *Revista das Academias de Letras*. Rio de Janeiro.

(1941) *História de Nísia Floresta*. Rio de Janeiro: Ed. Irmãos Potengi.

Castriciano, H. (1979) Uma figura literária do Nordeste. In *Nordeste*. Facsimile edition (introduction M. Mota; foreword G. Freyre). Recife: Arquivo Público Estadual/Secretaria da Justiça.

Clarke, D. M., trans. and ed. (2013) *The Equality of the Sexes: Three Feminist Texts of the Seventeenth Century*. Oxford: Oxford University Press.

Darnton, R. (2021) *Pirating and Publishing: The Book Trade in the Age of the Enlightenment*. New York: Oxford University Press.

Diniz, F. Senhorinha da Motta. (1873) A educação da mulher [editorial essay]. *O Sexo Feminino: Semanario Dedicado aos Interesses da Mulher*, 1(1), September 7. http://memoria.bn.br/pdf/706868/per706868_1873_00001.pdf.

Doria, E. (1933) Nísia Floresta. *Revista da Semana*, 48, 16. http://memoria .bn.br/DocReader/DocReader.aspx?bib=025909_03&hf=memoria.bn .br&pagfis=8722.

Dorlin, E. (2001) *L'évidence de l'égalité des sexes: Une philosophie oubliée du XVIIe siècle*. Paris: L'Harmattan.

Duarte, C. L. (1989) Introdução. In Nísia Floresta Brasileira Augusta. *Direitos das Mulheres e Injustiça dos Homens*. São Paulo: Cortez Editora.

(1990) Nos primórdios do feminismo brasileiro: Direitos das mulheres e injustiça dos homens. In Nádia B. Gotlib (ed.). *A mulher na literatura*, vol. III (pp. 38–41). Belo Horizonte: Imprensa da UFMG.

(1995) *Nísia Floresta: Vida e obra*. Natal: Ed. UFRN.

(1999) Revendo o indianismo brasileiro: A lágrima de um Caeté, de Nísia Floresta. *Revista do Centro de Estudos Portugueses*, 19(25), 153–177. www .periodicos.letras.ufmg.br/index.php/cesp/article/view/6799/5793.

(2019) *#Nísia Floresta Presente: Uma brasileira ilustre*. Natal: Mariana Hardi.

(2021) Ainda o Enigma: Revendo os primórdios do feminismo brasileiro. In Nísia Floresta Brasileira Augusta, *Direitos das Mulheres e Injustiça dos Homens*. Natal: Sertão das Letras Edições.

Ferguson, M., ed. (1985) *First Feminists: British Women Writers 1578–1799*. Bloomington: Indiana University Press.

Franco, A. A. de Melo (1976) *O índio brasileiro e a Revolução Francesa*. 2nd ed. Rio de Janeiro: José Olympio; Brasília: INL.

Freire, P. (1993) *The Pedagogy of the Oppressed*. New York: Continuum.

Freyre, G. (1936/2006) *Sobrados e Mucambos*. São Paulo: Global.

Gardeton, C. (1876) (trans.) *Les Droits des femmes, et l'injustice des hommes; par Mistriss Godwin. Traduit librement de l'anglais, sur la huitième édition; augmenté d'un apologue: L'instruction sert aux femmes à trouver des maris. Par M. César Gardeton, auteur du Dictionnaire de la beauté, etc., etc.* Paris: L. F. Hivert, libraire, rue des Mathurins Saint-Jacques, n° 18.

Garnier, C. (1987) "La Femme n'est pas inférieure à l'homme" (1750): œuvre de Madeleine Darsant de Puisieux ou simple traduction française? *Revue d'Histoire littéraire de la France*, 87(4), 709–713.

Green, K. (2020) Catharine Macaulay. In E. N. Zalta (ed.), *The Stanford Encyclopedia of Philosophy* (Summer Edition). https://plato.stanford.edu/ entries/catharine-macaulay/.

Johnson, N. (2020) Early Critical Reception. In N. Johnson & P. Keen (eds.), *Mary Wollstonecraft in Context* (pp. 41–49). Cambridge: Cambridge University Press. https://doi.org/10.1017/9781108261067.

Koster, H. (1816) *Travels in Brazil*. London: Longman, Hurst, Rees, Orme, and Brown.

Leduc, G. (2010) *Réécritures anglaises au XVIIIe siècle de "l'Égalité des deux sexes" (1673) de François Poulain de la Barre: Du politique au polemique*. Paris: L'Harmattan.

(2015) Stylistic Desacralisation of Man in Britain in the Sophia Pamphlets (1739–1740). In P. Partenza (ed.), *Dynamics of Desacralization: Disenchanted Literary Talents* (pp. 13–35). Goettingen: VandRunipress.

Lima, O. (1919) *Nísia Floresta*. Rio de Janeiro: Revista do Brasil, dez.

Lúcio, S. V. M. (1999) Uma Viajante Brasileira na Itália do Risorgimento: Tradução comentada do livro Trois Ans En Italie Suivis D'un Voyage en Grèce (Vol I – 1864; Vol II – s.d) de Nísia Floresta Brasileira Augusta. PhD thesis, State University of Campinas.

Margutti, P. (2017) Nísia Floresta e a questão da autoria de Direitos das mulheres, injustiças dos homens. *Annales*, 2(3), 5–23.

(2019) *Nísia Floresta, uma Brasileira desconhecida: Feminismo, positivismo e outras tendências*. Porto Alegre: Editora Fi.

Matthews, C. H. (2010) Between "Founding Text" and "Literary Prank": Reasoning the Roots of Nísia Floresta's *Direitos das Mulheres e Injustiça dos Homens. Ellipsis*, 8, 9–36. https://jls.apsa.us/index.php/jls/article/view/99/120.

(2012) *Gender, Race and Patriotism in the Works of Nísia Floresta*. Woodbridge, UK: Tamesis.

Moore, C. A. (1916) The First of the Militants in English Literature. *The Nation*, 102, 194–196.

Nascimento, B. (1985) O Conceito de quilombo e a resistência cultural negra. *Afrodiáspora: Revista do Mundo Negro*, 6–7, 41–49.

O Correio da manhã. (1954) Nísia Floresta Uma Figura Romântica, September 4. http://memoria.bn.br/pdf/089842/per089842_1954_18856.pdf.

O Mercantil. (1847) Instrucção Publica – Revista dos Collegios da Capital. II, January 17. http://memoria.bn.br/docreader/DocReader.aspx?bib=228133&pagfis=3465.

O'Brien, K. (2009) *Women and Enlightenment in Eighteenth-Century Britain*. New York: Cambridge University Press.

Pallares-Burke, M. L. G. (1996) A Mary Wollstonecraft que o Brasil conheceu, ou a travessura literária de Nísia Floresta. In *Nísia Floresta: O carapuceiro e outros ensaios da tradução cultural* (pp. 167–192). São Paulo: Hucitec.

(2021) Nísia Floresta: Revisitando seu papel na história das ideias feministas e educacionais. Vozes: Mulheres na História da Filosofia Conference, Federal University of Rio de Janeiro, May 3. www.youtube.com/watch?v=ccXYMCCVVcE&t=13s.

Pohl, N. & Schellenberg, B. (2003) *Reconsidering the Bluestockings*. San Marino: University of California Press.

Popkin, R. (1979) *The History of Scepticism from Erasmus to Spinoza*. Berkeley: University of California Press.

Poulain de la Barre, F. (1677) *The Woman As Good As the Man: Or, the Equality of Both Sexes* (trans. A. L.). London: T. M. for N. Brooks. https://quod .lib.umich.edu/e/eebo/A55529.0001.001?view=toc.

Reuter, M. (2019) François Poulain de la Barre. In E. N. Zalta (ed.), *The Stanford Encyclopedia of Philosophy.* https://plato.stanford.edu/archives/ win2019/entries/francois-barre/.

Secco, G. & Pugliese, N. (in press) Teaching Nísia Floresta: Mapping the Philosophical Grounds. In R. Hagengruber (ed.), *Teaching Women Philosophers with Concepts*. Cham: Springer.

Schmitter, A. M. (2018) Cartesian Prejudice: Gender, Education and Authority in Poulain de la Barre. *Philosophy Compass*, 13(12), 1–12.

Seidl, R. (1938). *Nísia Floresta: 1810–1885*. Rio de Janeiro [publisher unknown].

Sharpe, P. (1989) Introdução. In Nísia Floresta, *Opúsculo Humanitário* (introduction and notes P. Sharpe-Valadares). São Paulo: Cortez Editora.

(1995). Nisia Floresta: "Woman" (including Livia A. de Faria's English translation of Floresta's essay). *BRASIL/BRAZIL: A Journal of Brazilian Literature*, 83–120. Brown Digital Repository, Brown University Library. https://doi.org/10.26300/847a-p309.

Soares, Erica. (2017) Copie assumée, copie dissumulée: Les racines controversées de Diretos das mulheres e injustiça dos homens de Nísia Floresta. Master's thesis, University of Toulouse II Jean Jaurès.

Sophia (1739) *Woman Not Inferior to Man or, a Short and Modest Vindication of the Natural Right of the Fair-Sex to a Perfect Equality of Power, Dignity, and Esteem, with Men*. London: John Hawkings.

Wollstonecraft, M. (2016) *Reivindicação do direito das mulheres* (trans. I. Pocinho Motta). São Paulo: Boitempo.

Ximenes, S. B. (2019) Apresentação da Obra. In *Cinco Obras Completas de Nísia Floresta Brasileira Augusta*. E-book. Kindle. www.amazon.com.br/ Cinco-Obras-Completas-Primeira-digital-ebook/dp/B082S51YXZ.

Cambridge Elements ☰

Women in the History of Philosophy

Jacqueline Broad
Monash University

Jacqueline Broad is Associate Professor of Philosophy at Monash University, Australia. Her area of expertise is early modern philosophy, with a special focus on seventeenth and eighteenth-century women philosophers. She is the author of *Women Philosophers of the Seventeenth Century* (Cambridge University Press, 2002), *A History of Women's Political Thought in Europe, 1400–1700* (with Karen Green; Cambridge University Press, 2009), and *The Philosophy of Mary Astell: An Early Modern Theory of Virtue* (Oxford University Press, 2015).

About the Series

In this Cambridge Elements series, distinguished authors provide concise and structured introductions to a comprehensive range of prominent and lesser-known figures in the history of women's philosophical endeavour, from ancient times to the present day.

Cambridge Elements $^{\equiv}$

Women in the History of Philosophy

Elements in the Series

Pythagorean Women
Caterina Pellò

Frances Power Cobbe
Alison Stone

Olympe de Gouges
Sandrine Bergès

Simone de Beauvoir
Karen Green

Im Yunjidang
Sungmoon Kim

Early Christian Women
Dawn LaValle Norman

Mary Shepherd
Antonia LoLordo

Mary Wollstonecraft
Martina Reuter

Susan Stebbing
Frederique Janssen-Lauret

Victoria Welby
Emily Thomas

Harriet Taylor Mill
Helen McCabe

Nísia Floresta
Nastassja Pugliese

A full series listing is available at: www.cambridge.org/EWHP